THE KITCHEN GARDEN

'This book, written by an acknowledged authority on vegetables, is well illustrated, up to date and excellent value for money.' *The Observer*

'Difficult to find better value . . . the varieties named are a true indication that the writer is abreast of the times.' *The Birmingham Post*

'This is the sort of book for the back gardener who wants to grow his own vegetables, grow them well and grow them with the minimum of trouble.' *The Northern Gardener*

BRIAN FURNER is a Fellow of the Linnean Society of London and a member of the Soil Association. In the gardening world he is well known as a vegetable specialist—all the vegetables he eats are grown on his own allotment in Kent—and in particular as an exponent of up-to-date, labour-saving methods. He has studied horticulture as far afield as Israel and Morocco and keeps in touch with research stations in the USA and Russia.

D0207622

Pan Piper Small Garden Series
Editor: C. E. Lucas Phillips

THE KITCHEN GARDEN

BRIAN FURNER

Revised Edition
A PAN ORIGINAL

PAN BOOKS LTD : LONDON

First published 1966 by
PAN BOOKS LTD
33 Tothill Street, London, S.W.1

ISBN 0 330 23109 X

2nd Printing, 1971

PRINTED IN ENGLAND BY
HAZELL WATSON AND VINEY LTD
AYLESBURY, BUCKS

CONTENTS

PART ONE

PART TWO

ILLUSTRATIONS
IN PHOTOGRAVURE

Golden Boy tomatoes have a fine flavour, and weigh up to 1 lb
each
Sweet Peppers harvested from plants in the author's cold frame
Sutton's Smallpak is a new bush type vegetable marrow
Save space by gardening vertically

LINE DRAWINGS

PART ONE

CHAPTER I

THE BEGINNINGS

THIS book has but one aim – to help you grow healthy, nourishing food for the family. If you already do so, you are a good gardener and you may pass over a good deal of this book, but I hope that it may still help you to be a better one and to grow a wider variety with economy of effort.

There is nothing in this book to assist you to grow yard-long beans or spuds as big as footballs. It is no more than a guide on how to produce a good range of vegetables the year through. You will also want to produce the crops cheaply. That point has been borne in mind – although there are, of course, initial expenses for tools and accessories. Those who are new to gardening will no doubt be pleased to know that the production of nutritious, flavoursome vegetables does not involve the use of unpleasant and possibly dangerous poison sprays and powders.

Far too many people want everything to be easy these days. The growing of fine crops of vegetables is not all that difficult but calls for some work, practice and a great deal of common sense. Do not overdo the work side of kitchen gardening – especially in bad weather. Gardening certainly helps keep down the waistline, but you can overdo things. In this book you will find some suggestions which may help you to reduce back-aching jobs to the minimum.

Orthodox methods are ideal providing you have the right type of soil, adequate time to carry out the work, animal manure and fertilizers in quantity and a knowledge of soil chemistry. The suggestions in this book are indeed based on orthodox methods but I have kept in mind the fact that, like me, you are an amateur gardener – not a professional. You will, however, find a great deal about some modern techniques, especially the use of cloches and black polythene. I hope you will come to regard these as normal practice, not as specialists' gadgets. Such garden aids can make all the difference. You may see advertisements for plastic cloches; by all means try them, but experience has shown that, for our kinds of job, no good substitute has yet been found for glass.

Around £10 will cover the cost of the more essential tools. These are a spade, a digging fork, a draw hoe, a Dutch (pushing type) hoe, a rake, a trowel, a small hand fork, a watering can fitted with one or two 'roses' (especially a fine rose), a dibber and a garden line.

To make a start you need a spade, a digging fork and a garden line. There is no need to buy a line, which is simply a piece of wire or rope tied to two pieces of wood or steel. When buying tools, be sure that they are of the best quality. A tool that breaks in one's hands is money wasted.

A specimen seed order is shown on page 30. This gives some idea of the annual outlay each spring, amply sufficient to keep a family well supplied with good vegetables for the year. Some gardeners will not be able to accommodate all these crops and obviously you will cut out any that you don't care for. On the other hand you may want to add some of those mentioned in the chapter 'Epicure's Choice'.

As far as manures and fertilizers are concerned, how much you will spend on them depends a great deal on you. If you can buy farmyard or stable manure cheaply, you are one of the few fortunate gardeners in Britain today. Some local authorities sell composted household refuse at a reasonable price. Other suitable materials are also offered for sale. Garden compost costs nothing but you have to make it yourself and you need quite a lot of it. Fertilizers do not replace manure or compost. If you already use or intend to use factory-made chemical fertilizers, use a complete fertilizer like Growmore or, better still, natural fertilizers made from bones, seaweed or apple pulp.

This book is divided into three parts. Part 1 helps the beginner to make a start and suggests how to manage the kitchen garden, feed its soil and enjoy oneself without doing too much work. In Part 2 all the main vegetables grown in the kitchen garden are discussed in detail. In Chapters XIV and XV you will meet some less common vegetables and a few herbs. Part 3 links up with Part 1 in offering further help and it deals with greenhouse food crops as well as something about the many friends and some enemies likely to be met in the garden. If, like so many these days, your garden is on a new housing estate and is pitifully small, read in Part 3 how food crops can be grown in pocket-handkerchief-sized plots.

Right at the back will be found some short appendices on the year's work, on gardening jargon and a short list of recommended seedsmen. I particularly ask you to turn to Appendix B unless you are already familiar with gardening terms. All trades have their own particular jargon and it is very important that we should have a clear idea of the language that is our common usage. Words like 'spit', 'bolt' and others may not appear polite to your maiden aunt, but they are the common currency of gardeners and have their special meanings.

The photographs which illustrate this book were taken in my own garden and I am grateful to boys of Slade Green (Kent) Secondary School for their help with the sketches.

CHAPTER II

THE SOIL AND ITS MANAGEMENT

SOIL is a thin, loose layer formed from the outer crust of rock of our planet. If you were to dig a deep trench – or better still watch somebody else digging one – you would notice that the soil varies in colour and texture. The top layer is generally darker and full of roots. Lower down, the soil is compact, lighter in colour and pretty lifeless. As gardeners, we are more concerned with the top layer, known as top soil. This may be several feet deep if you live in Lincolnshire or no deeper than six inches, as in my garden. Mismanagement of the top soil spells disaster to our crops, so it is very much in our interest to preserve and enrich it.

Topsoil is made up of minerals, plant and animal matter, water and air. The plant and animal matter is often referred to as the organic content – at other times as humus. The topsoil is also the home of many unseen bacteria, fungi and viruses. Research workers tell us that a small spoonful of topsoil contains twice as many microscopic organisms as there are people in the world. It is in the topsoil that we meet many friendly and a few less friendly insects; some of them are mentioned in Part 3.

Soil Types

Soils are classified according to their dominant ingredient. Chalky soils occur on top of limestone and chalk deposits; sandy soils are loose and gritty and are known as light soils. Clay soils are called heavy – probably because digging them is such hard work. Peat soils are dark and, like clay soils, often need drainage. Good garden soil is made up of sand, clay, a little chalk and possibly some peat.

If you have recently moved into a new home on one of the new housing estates, the soil in the garden may look pretty hopeless. Do not worry. Within a year or two you will be growing vegetables of which you will be justly proud. Here, in brief, is how to set about improving a soil.

Sandy and chalky soils are hungry. To feed them, we add bulky organic matter such as farmyard manure, garden compost, wool shoddy and autumn leaves. Bulky organic manures assist the water-holding capacity of a light soil. In a heavy soil, the same materials improve drainage. Clay and peat soils benefit from liming and are enriched by manure and compost.

Lime

Many newcomers to vegetable gardening may gain the impression from old hands that lime must be added to the soil each autumn or winter. This is quite wrong. Some soils have such a high chalk content that they do not need any liming at all. What does lime do ?

The element calcium is itself a plant food and, in the presence of calcium carbonate (chalk, limestone), chemical reactions in the soil release phosphorous and potassium, which are also very important plant foods, from insoluble compounds. Lime also counteracts excess acidity in the soil. This is very important in vegetable gardens where the soil type is peat or where a great deal of animal manure is used in the garden. In a clay soil, lime exerts a physical change which permits water and air to enter the soil more easily. In sandy soils, lime binds the soil particles together, preventing water from draining quickly away.

Only a chemical analysis of the soil can prove if and how much lime is needed. Most gardeners, who understand what lime does, treat the matter in a common-sense manner. They rotate their crops as explained in Chapter IV and, following the plan, they spread ground chalk over the soil at the rate of $\frac{1}{4}$ lb to the square yard.

Never lime the plot in which potatoes are to be planted in the spring. The potato plant prefers a soil which is slightly acid. Liming generally follows winter digging.

Where lime is added to the compost heap (see next chapter) there may be no need to lime at all. A soil rich in earthworms may not need lime. Worms not only prefer soils which suit our vegetables but the excreta of worms, known as casts, is rich in lime and other plant foods.

The Initial Clearance

If you inherit a weed-infested garden, you may well feel that a clean sweep should be made. Before investing in a flame thrower or building a supersized bonfire, bear in mind that the weed growth contains within it a great deal of soil fertility. There, locked up in the grass and weeds, are nitrogen, potassium, phosphorous, calcium, iron, manganese and a host of other chemicals our plants need. Burn the weeds and you will lose a great many chemicals in smoke.

Far better to slice off the top two inches of sod and weeds and leave the pile to rot down. Within two to three years, the stuff will resemble good potting compost which you may spread on top of the ground. In the meantime, you will have dug your soil and harvested some reasonably good crops. Taking over a very weedy garden calls for a great deal of work during the first two seasons. The hoe and the fork must be used actively.

Why We Dig

Orthodox gardeners continue to dig and double dig. We dig for several good reasons. Weeds must be cleared from the ground before we sow or plant and the action of digging loosens the soil so that rain enters it easily. Sometimes a hard layer forms a foot or so beneath the surface. This layer is broken by the spade. Disturbing the soil by digging also disturbs insect pests living in it. It is also believed that the soil benefits from being aerated during the digging process.

The best time for digging is between September and Christmas. Do not dig if the soil is soaking wet or frozen and do not attempt to break down the soil to a fine 'tilth' when doing so. Leave the clods on the surface. Winter frosts will break them down for you and you may then rake level and fine, ready for sowing in early spring.

How to Dig

Orthodox gardening lists four kinds of digging operations – trenching, bastard trenching, ridging and plain surface digging. For these operations the spade is used. Vacant land is generally forked over in spring before sowing and planting. The fork is also used in summer and autumn when ground is being prepared for a new crop.

How deeply you dig and how often depends on your soil. In trenching, the soil is disturbed to a depth of three spits. It is extremely hard work and although the trained gardener may be able to make a good job of it, I do not recommend the amateur to try. Bastard trenching, also known as Double Digging, is carried out as explained in the next paragraph, but for the fact that the soil in the second spit down is turned over and loosened with the *fork*. The ground is manured during the operation and the manure is mixed into both the second and the top spit. Ridging is aimed at exposing clay soil to the beneficial action of severe winter frosts.

For most of us Plain Digging is hard enough work. Here is how to do it properly. Take out a trench about 15 in wide. Then dig out the next row of soil with the spade and throw it forward into the empty trench – and so on, row by row. Try to keep the spade as vertical as you can so that you dig down to about 10 in. If you are manuring during Plain Digging, lay the manure at the bottom of the initial trench. Subsequently, throw the dung on to the sloping surface of the row in front of you, covering it as you dig the next row. When the digging has been completed, a vacant trench will confront you. Fill this with the soil dug out to make the initial trench at the far end of the garden. Whilst digging, although (providing you can recognize them) you may safely dig in all young annual weeds, remove all weeds with long tap roots and every piece of plant and root of such garden horrors as ground elder, bindweed and couch grass. Annual weeds which are at the flowering stage or which have made seed heads must also be removed.

If you decide to dig your soil more deeply than the 10 in depth of Plain Digging, take great care that you do not bring poor quality subsoil to the surface. Good crops cannot be expected where the subsoil is brought to the top.

Organic Surface Cultivation

Digging is not so popular as it was and organic surface cultivation has received quite a lot of publicity in recent years. The spade is not used at all. One group of gardeners makes use of the fork and the hoe to cultivate the top few inches. Others – the 'No Diggers' – do not disturb the soil at all and the few weeds which germinate in the rich but sawdust-mulched soil are pulled out by hand.

If you feel like trying organic surface cultivation in your garden, it is imperative that the soil is quite free of perennial weeds. Regular digging should continue until these weeds have been eliminated. Good, regular cultivation in spring and summer involves the removal of every new shoot of perennial weeds, as well, of course, of all other weed growth. If you use chemical weed killers (and I do not advise their use among food crops), do take great care that they do not touch your vegetable plants. Use the chemicals strictly to the manufacturer's instructions.

In this short book, I can deal in only a cursory way with the nature of soil and the methods of its cultivation. These points are dealt with much more fully in another book of this Pan Piper series – *The Small Garden* by C. E. Lucas Phillips.

CHAPTER III

FEEDING THE SOIL

MANURE – COMPOST MAKING – FERTILIZERS

G ARDENING is an unnatural practice and the more zealously we cultivate our garden, the greater the loss of soil fertility. In the past, well-rotted farmyard or stable manure was used to maintain and to increase the fertility of the garden. The manure not only supplied plant foods but it improved the soil's structure. Heavy soils were opened up and their cultivation was made easier. Light soils were bound together, erosion was prevented and less moisture lost.

Manure

But we live in the age of the diesel and petrol engine and few of us in towns even see a horse other than on television. Cow manure may be available in large quantities in areas where dairy farming is practised but most dairymen haul the manure back to the fields for the production of animal foodstuffs. Rotted animal manure – whether horse, cow or pig should not be used too liberally. A heaped barrow-load is estimated as about right for a 30 ft row. This works out (so I am told, although I have never checked it) at about a pailful to the square yard. Fresh manure should be stacked and left to ferment. If you can add several times its weight of vegetable wastes to it and ferment the mixture, so much the better. Always stack or store manure under some form of cover.

Rabbit, guinea pig, sheep, pigeon and poultry droppings are best used as activators for the compost heap or used as fertilizers.

As alternatives to animal manure, many gardeners use wool

shoddy, treated sewage, spent hops, municipal compost and proprietary preparations.

Compost Making

Providing you are willing to spend the money on kitchen gardening as you would on any other hobby, by all means buy manure or a substitute. The gardener aiming at providing the family with a supply of home-grown vegetables at little cost will prefer to use a substitute which costs nothing at all. This is garden compost. There is nothing new about its use. Chinese farmers and gardeners have been making compost for thousands of years. I have used nothing but compost in my own garden for sixteen years and my results demonstrate its great value.

Garden compost is made by fermenting waste materials in heaps and there are different ways of doing this. The best known method is the Indore Process (not 'indoor'), invented by the late Sir Albert Howard. 6-in thick layers of vegetable wastes are covered with a 2-in thick layer of animal manure. A sprinkling of chalk is made over each layer of vegetable matter. All dry material is wetted and hard plant stalks are bruised and broken. For gardeners with no source of animal manure, special proprietary compost making powders are on offer at garden shops and chain stores. Instructions on how to use the preparations is given on the packets.

My own way of making garden compost is rather haphazard. All waste materials are added to make a heap which is finally at least two yards square and 5 ft high. No lime is added and if no pigeon, rabbit or guinea pig droppings are to hand, no manure is included. All of the wastes are reasonably moist and I try to complete a heap within a month of starting it. This is never possible during the winter when there is a dearth of suitable waste materials. When finished, the heap is weighed down by an inch layer of top soil. The heap is then covered with a large sheet of black polythene.

Fermentation starts immediately and the compost is ready for use within from one to five months – depending on the time of the year. A spring-made heap, containing a great deal of sappy material, rots down very quickly. The heaps are not turned. Any woody plant remains or pieces of clothing and newsprint which have not disintegrated are added to the new heap.

Failures in compost making are due to the fact that the gardener has not realised that conditions must suit the bacteria which do the work. A good mixture is the first essential and there must be sufficient moisture. In the early stages of decomposition, some air must be present, so the heap must not be too compact. The bacteria need plenty of nitrogen. This is obtained from animal manure, sappy greenstuff or the special compost making compounds.

Every effort must be made to conserve the heat engendered during the process and the new black plastic idea replaces the rugs, mats, sacks, carpets and tarpaulin sheets used as covers in the past.

The owner of a small garden may not be able to obtain large quantities of waste materials in a short time. Heaps made rather slowly over a period of several months should be housed in a bin or box. Suitable measurements are a yard square and a yard high. All compost heaps must stand on soil, so no special base is needed. As and when materials are added, they should be covered with a sprinkling of soil. The heap must always be covered to protect the contents from heavy rain and snow.

Although one may truthfully say that anything which has lived may be composted, there are certain waste materials which are best omitted. I am thinking of dead animals, slaughterhouse offal, human excreta, prickly prunings from rose and blackberry bushes and anything hard and woody that will not rot quickly.

Here are most of the ingredients you are likely to come across and which are suitable for composting:

Soft hedge cuttings and leaves, wet hay, semi-rotted straw,

sawdust and wood shavings in small quantities, newspapers and waste paper, weeds and their roots but not the roots of perennials, all garden plants after crops have been harvested, kitchen and household wastes, animal manures in small quantities, unsold fruit and vegetables from the greengrocer or the supermarket and spent hops, leather dust and wool wastes from factories.

When fermentation is nearing completion manure worms in their thousands breed in the heap and break down the materials. The earthworm does not enter the compost heap.

Perhaps you are wondering why we do not simply dig all waste materials into the soil. This could be done and the soil would be enriched in due course, but, because all available nitrogen in the soil would be seized by the soil bacteria for the decomposition of the wastes, the soil itself would be de-nitrified until rotting was completed. There would also be no heating up and it is the heat which kills weed seeds and the organisms on diseased plant wastes.

Garden compost may be dug into the soil or simply spread on to it. The compost may be applied at any time of the year, providing the soil is damp but not frozen. How much compost you apply depends on how much you make. A pailful to the square yard is generally recommended, but a barrowload is far better.

If sifted, garden compost also provides an excellent potting mixture for raising vegetables from seeds.

Municipal composts and other materials. Where municipal compost is purchased from a local authority, use it at the rates of application suggested by the makers. Sewage may have been used in its preparation, making the mixture far richer than home-made garden compost. Before seaweed is applied to the soil, excess salt should be washed from it. Do this by spreading out the seaweed and exposing it to rain. Use wet seaweed at the rate of 2 pailfuls to the square yard. Treated sewage should be used sparingly and a shovelful to the square yard should be sufficient. Wastes from breweries and woollen mills and carpet factories are not considered as complete substitutes for animal manure and are best treated as soil improvers.

Fertilizers

All manures are soil conditioners and plants feed in the enriched soil. Fertilizers may be compared to tonics and vitamin pills. A fertilizer may be organic (obtained from animal or vegetable remains) or inorganic (from deposits in the ground or factory-made). There are many kinds of fertilizers containing different chemical salts or different quantities of the salts. A mixed fertilizer like Growmore contains salts of the three main plant foods – nitrogen, phosphorous and potassium. Natural fertilizers contain several plant foods, with one, at times, predominating.

In the same way that our bodies do not need vitamin pills if we eat sufficient healthy food, so our vegetable plants do not need fertilizers if the soil is fed regularly. If you have just taken over a garden where the soil is so poor that you have no hope of producing anything worth while, fertilizers can help you providing you use them with great care. A strong dose of any fertilizer is liable to sicken your soil and ruin your vegetables. Where droppings from poultry and pigeons are to be used as a fertilizer, they should be dried and ground into powder and mixed with a little dry sand before being sprinkled around growing crops at the rate of 8 oz to the square yard. Other organic fertilizers like dried blood, hoof and horn meal, bone flour, fish meal and those made from seaweed or from apple pulp should be applied according to the supplier's instructions.

Liquid manure is a useful, home-made fertilizer. It is made by suspending a sack of animal manure in a tub or tank of water. Use at the rate of 1 pt to 1 qt in a gallon of water.

In addition to mixed or complete chemical fertilizers like Growmore, there are many others which contain but one plant

FIG. 1 Making liquid manure

food. Although these chemical fertilizers may be cheap to buy I do not advise their use except where the gardener is something of an expert. Bear in mind that the maximum dosage is generally very small – around $\frac{1}{2}$ oz to the square yard – and it is so easy to overdose and harm both your soil and your vegetables.

CHAPTER IV

WHAT TO GROW

I CANNOT come into your garden to study the amount of ground you can spare for vegetables and then plan a cropping programme for you. Were you to invite me to do so, I feel quite sure that you or your wife would disagree with many of my suggestions. After all, you will wish to grow the vegetables which you and your family like. I might mention parsnips – a vegetable many people cannot stomach. I might omit beetroot, which your wife may need for salads on and off throughout the year.

A Question of Space

Cropping plan. Although we live in the space age, as far as we gardeners are concerned, lack of space is our main problem. Another chapter deals with some of the problems of growing food crops in a modern, very small garden. For the purpose of this chapter, I am imagining that you have a medium to large garden and that quite a fair proportion of it is used for vegetables. I am not in favour of complicated cropping plans, because I am in no sense a planner. With experience one somehow knows approximately how much room each crop needs, although early June finds me running round the garden in search of a few vacant square feet in which to set out the last of the half-hardy plants from the cold frame. Until you can estimate how much room the principal crops, such as potatoes and cabbages, will need, I think it will help you if you make a rough plan of the garden in January before you order seeds and seed potatoes. If your plan is more or less to scale, you will see at a glance, after you have shaded in the potato and cabbage plots, about how much room will be available for the many other vegetables you wish to grow.

If you have not grown vegetables before, the following may help you to estimate the amount of space they require.

In 1 sq yd you may grow: 4 early potato plants *or* 3 lates *or* 4 cabbages of a compact variety *or* 2 medium-sized cabbages *or* 1 tall growing brussels sprouts plant *or* 2 dwarf brussels plants *or* 2 cauliflowers *or* 2 plants sprouting broccoli.

If you are starting from scratch in a new garden, leave sufficient room on your plan for a garden shed, a cold frame and a site for the manure or compost heap.

No kitchen garden is complete without fruit and because of the limited space in the modern back garden, fruit and vegetables are intermingled instead of being grown separately. When planning a new garden, decide how much room you have for soft fruits like strawberries, raspberries and currants. If there is sufficient space for a few cordon or dwarf apples and pears, so much the better; bear in mind that vegetables do not thrive in shade, but trees can provide a useful wind break if grown at the north side of the garden.

The Seed Order

January is the time to buy seeds and your local garden shop and the chain stores will have them for sale then. You may prefer to order from a specialist seed firm. You will find the names and addresses of several reputable seed firms in Appendix C. Most seed firms send catalogues free of charge but it seems polite to me to enclose return postage when asking the firms to do so. Study the catalogues carefully with your wife and discuss with her what you are thinking of growing. She will be cooking the produce and she knows the family's likes and dislikes.

If your garden is decidedly small, remember that the farmer grows good winter supplies of carrots, beetroots, parsnips, potatoes and cabbages, which are on sale at reasonable prices. Concentrate on vegetables which are far better if harvested from the garden but a few hours, or even minutes, before being eaten. Examples are radishes, lettuces and spring onions. Think, too, of vegetables which are more flavoursome when home-grown – peas, dwarf and runner beans, cauliflowers and tomatoes. If there is room, do try to grow a few early potatoes, not only because they are dug when shop prices are usually high but also because home-grown earlies have such a fine flavour.

Little known vegetables. Far too many seasoned gardeners are so conservative that even the names of the less common vegetables frighten them! If you are new to vegetable growing, I hope you will not fall victim to this strange attitude of mind. For goodness sake do not fill the garden with plants of the many vegetables discussed in Chapter XIV but do grow one or two of them each season.

Varieties and novelties. You will notice that a seedsman lists several different varieties of each vegetable. The varieties listed by one seedsman may be different from those offered in the catalogue of another firm. Then the seedsmen complicate things even more by adding 'Our own strain', 'Specially selected' and 'F.1 hybrid'. This is all very confusing to the beginner, who would be well advised to choose varieties which have proved their worth over the years. I have grown most of the varieties mentioned in Parts 2 and 3 and I have no hesitation in recommending them.

'F.1 Hybrids', by the way, are usually good value. They are varieties specially raised by controlled fertilization between two selected parents and the union is effected afresh every year.

Here is a specimen seed order for your guidance. Increase or decrease the potatoes according to the size of your garden.

Quantity	Vegetable	Variety	New pence
1 packet (½ pint)	Pea ⎤	*Choose a first early,*	11½
1 packet (½ pint)	Pea ⎬	*second early and a*	11½
1 packet (1 pint)	Pea ⎦	*maincrop variety*	22½
1 packet (½ pint)	Broad bean		11½
1 packet	Dwarf bean		12½
1 packet	Runner bean		12½
1 packet	Beet		6
1 packet	Brussels sprouts		6
1 packet	Sprouting broccoli		6
1 packet	Cauliflower		6
1 packet	Cauliflower broccoli		6
1 packet	Cabbage ⎤	*Choose a spring, a*	6
1 packet	Cabbage ⎬	*summer and a late-heading*	6
1 packet	Cabbage ⎦	*kind*	6
1 packet	Carrots		5
1 packet	Cucumber ⎤	*One variety for under glass*	7½
1 packet	Cucumber ⎦	*and one for outdoors*	7½
1 packet	Kale		5
1 packet	Leeks		6
1 packet	Lettuce ⎤	*Choose a cabbage and*	5
1 packet	Lettuce ⎦	*a cos variety*	5
1 packet	Melon		7½
1 packet	Onion (*for spring onions*)		5
1 packet	Parsnip		5
1 packet	Radish		5
1 packet (1 oz)	Spinach		6½
1 packet (1 oz)	Sweet corn		17½
1 packet	Tomato		7½
1 packet (1 oz)	Turnip		5
1 packet	Vegetable marrow		6
1 lb	Onion sets (*for maincrop onions*)		20
7 lb	Potato ⎤	*Choose a first early,*	49
14 lb	Potato ⎬	*a second early and a*	80
28 lb	Potato ⎦	*maincrop variety*	145

£5.30p

You can economize in several ways. Thus you may not need both dwarf and runner beans, nor true cauliflowers as well as cauliflower broccoli.

Some Gardening Practices

If you discuss your garden plan and your seed order with possibly more knowledgeable gardeners, they may ask you if you have taken rotation, intercropping, succession and catch-cropping into account. These are examples of good horticultural practice and they are frequently referred to in gardening magazines, so here is something about them.

Rotation of crops. All vegetables do not utilize the same amounts of plant foods in the soil. Where one vegetable has a liking for potash, another prefers more nitrogen. So, if we grow the same vegetable on the same plot of ground year after year, we shall very possibly exhaust the soil of one or more plant foods. It stands to reason, too, that if you grow the same vegetable in the same place for several years, there is every likelihood of a build-up of the pests and diseases to which that vegetable is subject. Thus a patch of soil may become cabbage-sick and infected with the dangerous club-root disease. To prevent these troubles from occurring, the gardener rotates his crops.

For the medium-sized garden, the following three-year plan is suggested. In a really large garden the rotation could be based on a four-year plan.

First Year	Second Year	Third Year
Potatoes	Brassicas (all kinds of cabbage)	Other vegetables
Soil manured or composted during winter digging.	*Soil limed, if necessary, in the autumn. Manured or composted later.*	*No manure or compost for root crops. A complete fertilizer may be applied just before sowing seeds.*

We may not be able to stick strictly to such a programme but any plan that is based on the practice of not growing the same vegetable in the same patch for two years running is a help.

Intercropping. This is a space-saver. Here are two examples. Lettuces are grown between rows of dwarf peas and plants of trailing vegetable marrows are guided through a block of sweet corn.

Succession. 'Successional sowing' means that one sows little and often throughout the season. Radishes and lettuces come to mind. 'Successional cropping' is quite different. Here one clears a piece of the garden from which a crop has been harvested as soon as one can. Another crop is then sown or planted at once. The idea is to keep the ground producing food and not to lie idle.

Catch cropping. Here again we make good use of every vacant square foot. You will reserve quite a large plot of ground for brussels sprouts and winter cabbage, but the plants will not be planted on the bed until June. Between March and June, use this plot for crops of lettuce and radish.

CHAPTER V

TO HELP YOU

THE chapter devoted to greenhouse food crops in Part 3 is to help you if you already have a greenhouse. I do not suggest that you buy one solely for the production of vegetables. The outlay just isn't worth the return. Cold frames and cloches cost less, are more versatile and are extremely valuable aids in the kitchen garden.

The Garden Frame

A cold frame consists of two parts – a box-like container and a glass lid usually called a 'light'. The box may be made of brick, cement, asbestos or wood. The light may be glass or clear plastic on a wooden framework. Gardeners are practical people and most of them make their own garden frames. If you prefer to buy one, there is a good range. Some modern designs consist of an all-steel or all-aluminium framework with glass panels at the sides. The light may be hinged or sliding.

Site and use. The garden frame should face due south and stand on the soil, which should be dug deeply so that all weed roots are removed. The top few inches of soil should be removed and replaced with a rich, sifted mixture of good garden soil and garden compost. John Innes Potting Compost No. 2 is also suitable.

The cold frame traps sun heat but, being almost airtight, the management of cold frames requires some thought regarding ventilation and shading. Common sense plays a very big part in both problems. During the winter keep the light closed at night and during frosty weather. Give as much ventilation as possible during the spring and summer. How much ventilation must be left to your judgement. This is something you learn with practice. If you raise plants of hardy vegetables like cabbage and lettuce in the frame, no harm will be done by leaving the light off the frame from mid-April onwards.

Seedlings and half-hardy plants need as much warmth as possible until hardening-off starts in late May. They need some ventilation, however, otherwise mildew or some other trouble will affect them. Special precautions must be taken to prevent a spring frost from damaging the plants. Covering the frame with sacking or with old rugs and carpets each evening is advisable if you feel there is likelihood of frost.

Shading. Now and then we have some sunshine during the summer months and frame-grown plants need a little shade to prevent scorching. Flecking a little whitewash on the glass is a great help.

A cold frame cropping plan. Here is how I use my own cold frames. How you will use yours will depend on what you wish to grow.

October to March	Cauliflower plants.
March to June	Sowings of lettuce and summer cabbage made in the bed in March. Sowings of half-hardy vegetables in April.
June to September	Tomatoes, melons and frame type cucumbers.

At times, the frames are also used for early strawberries and sweet peppers, as well as for drying-off onions and shallots in damp weather.

Cloches

The French word cloche means a bell and old-time cloches were bell-shaped. The modern continuous cloche was invented in 1912. Cloches vary in design from a simple tent, consisting of two sheets of glass, to the barn type with its special ventilating device. There are two sizes of barn cloches – the low barn and the large barn. In vegetable growing, the low barn is generally suitable but the large barn gives more headroom for the tomato crop.

Because cloches are not airtight, they need far less management as regards ventilation and, during very warm weather, one top panel of barn cloches may be fixed to allow the entry of more air or the glass sheet may be taken off without fear of the cloche collapsing. Rain, falling on to cloches, runs into the soil alongside them and the roots of cloche-grown plants (but not seedlings) make use of the water. This means that plants under cloches do not need watering so frequently as do plants growing in cold frames.

Cloches are light to handle and may be moved to all parts of the garden quite easily. The initial cost is quickly recovered providing the cloches are put to maximum use. Here is how this may be done.

Month	Sow or protect plants of:
January to June	Cabbage, cauliflower, broad beans, onions, lettuce, radish, peas, carrots, brussels sprouts, leeks, turnips, cucumbers, tomatoes, melons, French and runner beans, sweet corn, vegetable marrows.
June to September	Cucumbers, melons, tomatoes.
October to December	Cabbage, broad beans, lettuce, onions, spinach, peas.

Pots

The clay pot is popularly known as a flower pot. In vegetable growing other pots made of many different materials are worth considering. My own preference is for the peat pot and in Part 2 you will come across references as to the correct usage and handling of this kind of pot. You may have already tried paper, polythene or mulch pots. If they suit you, I have no wish to influence you towards peat pots.

Potting compost. Notice that there are two meanings of the word 'compost'. One we have seen. The other is a mixture of different soil components for raising seed or for pot plants. First-class results cannot be expected in the raising of plants from seed unless a good compost is used. I use sifted compost from my garden heap. Many gardeners rely on the special John Innes mixtures and for the raising of vegetable plants generally, I feel that John Innes Potting Compost No. 1 is suitable. This consists of sterilized loam, peat, sand, chalk and very small amounts of chemical salts. A great deal depends on your source of supply. I understand that the J.I. composts offered for sale by some garden shops are not always up to scratch.*

Water

During the summer months vegetables need a great deal of water. In the eastern half of the country, the rainfall is seldom sufficient. Some people object to the use of mains water because they feel that rain water is so much better. They are possibly right, but far better to use mains water than no water at all! You have to pay the water company a little extra for a garden tap and a sprinkler system is a good investment.

When using the watering can, do supply sufficient water to soak the soil. If you simply wet the top inch, you may do more harm than good. When watering seedlings, always use a very fine rose on the can. If you don't, your seedlings may be washed away!

Mulching

A mulch is a soil cover. Mulches play a very important part in my kitchen garden. Their virtues are many. They

prevent loss of soil moisture,
suppress many weeds,

*J.I. Composts are not proprietary articles; they are formulae devised by the John Innes Horticultural Institute.

prevent the soil from compacting after heavy rain,
insulate the soil from climatic temperature extremes,
protect the roots of plants from damage by the hoe, etc.,
save time, work and water, and
if the material is of an organic nature, the mulch decomposes slowly and enriches the soil.

As with all good things, mulches must be used correctly. Here are examples of what may happen if the gardener misuses a mulch:

If you lay down a mulch in early spring, the soil may be slow to warm up. The exception is a black polythene mulch over potatoes.

If you apply a mulch to a dry soil, the soil remains dry and may become even drier.

Unless your garden is the home of blackbirds and thrushes and possibly a hedgehog, slugs may thrive below mulches.

All kinds of materials come in handy for mulching – manure, garden compost, lawn mowings, straw, autumn leaves, sawdust, wood shavings, sedge peat, stones, newspapers, old sacks, rugs and carpets, black polythene sheeting.

Now that we've discussed a good many, rather general points on vegetable growing, it is time to get down to the sowing, planting and harvesting of the fine crops we intend to produce.

PART TWO

In the following pages you will read how the principal vegetable crops grown in our gardens are cultivated. Harvesting and storing, where applicable, are mentioned and although pests and diseases are covered by a special chapter in Part 3, where a vegetable is rather prone to attack by a specific pest or disease, a reference is made to the trouble in the next few chapters. Good use of cold frames and cloches is explained together with suggestions on how to use mulches to save you time and work. Manuring or composting and planning should follow the three-year rotation shown on page 31.

There is something about herbs in Chapter XV.

CHAPTER VI

PEAS AND BEANS

PEAS — BROAD BEANS — DWARF BEANS
RUNNER BEANS

Peas and beans belong to the legume family, all characterised by their elongated seed-pods. They are plants which make use of atmospheric nitrogen. To obtain the nitrogen, they have pinhead-sized knobs, containing nitrogen-making bacteria, on their roots. Nitrogen is an important plant food. After peas and beans have finished cropping, although the bine is removed and composted, the roots may be left to disintegrate in the soil. It is believed that by doing this a supply of available nitrogen is supplied to the follow-on crop.

Peas

All gardeners seem to agree that peas take up a lot of space. They do, but, as explained in Part 1, the vacant ground between the rows may be used for other crops, such as lettuce.

If you know very little about vegetable growing, you may be baffled when you study the list of pea varieties in the seedsman's catalogue. There are two main divisions – the round-seeded and the marrowfats or wrinkled. The round-seeded are reputed to be hardier and the wrinkled contain more sugar and so in general estimation have a better flavour. There are short, medium and tall varieties and because some take less time to come into crop, the varieties are grouped into three categories – First Early, Second Early and Maincrop, in which we may include the so-called Late varieties.

In theory, we should be able to sow several different varieties in early April and have the rows coming into bearing from late

June until August. I find this does not happen. The plants of a First Early variety come into bearing well in advance of the others. Then the weather seems to suit peas and all the plants suddenly develop pods which are ready for the pot in no time. Such a position suits one's relatives, friends and neighbours, with whom one shares one's bumper crop!

In practice it is wiser to sow on and off between mid to late March and early May. Cloches come in handy for the first sowing. Sow a second early during the first two weeks of April, a maincrop a week to ten days later and a late pea in May.

The growing of late peas is somewhat of a gamble. Even though you may keep the plants well supplied with water mildew often takes over and you find you have worked for nothing. Some people suggest sowing a first early variety in June or early July for peas in September and October. I have tried this – very unsuccessfully!

Sowing. If you already grow peas you may be quite happy with your way of doing so. The way I suggest here is one which I have found successful for many years. The soil will have been dug during the winter. Before raking the bed level, fork the soil to a depth of 2 or 3 in if rain or snow has compacted it. Distances between the rows are generally based on the height to which the plants grow, but I find that $2\frac{1}{2}$ ft between early and shorter maincrop varieties sufficient. Add a generous 6 in if you grow tall kinds. Use the garden line to ensure that your rows will be straight and make flat-bottomed trenches 2 in deep with the draw hoe.

Sprinkle the seeds as evenly as possible in three rows in these little trenches so that each seed is about 3 in from its neighbour. Rake soil over the seeds to fill the trench.

Staking and protection. Cloches give protection against birds to the earliest sowing but traps should be laid if mice are a menace. Later sowings made in the open must be protected

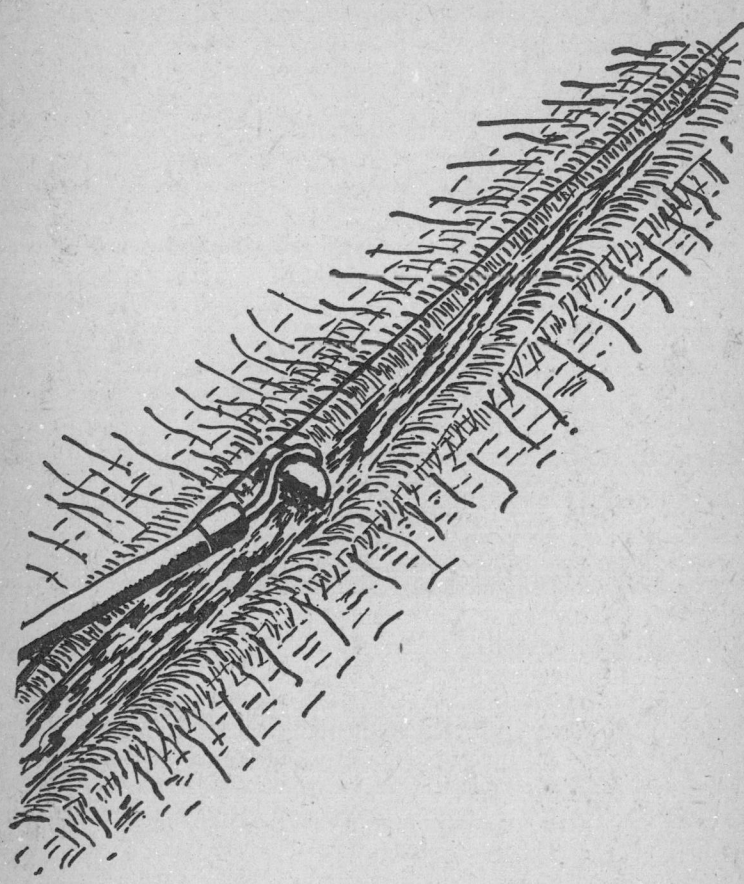

FIG. 2 Making 2 in deep, flat-bottomed trenches with the draw
hoe

from birds. Black cotton stretched over the rows gives good protection. Pea plants are natural climbers and the brushwood pea-sticks sold in shops are ideal. The twigs should be set on either side of the row. Failing brushwood, wire mesh is suitable.

For supporting plants growing no higher than 3 ft, I link the protection from birds with supports for the plants. Bamboo canes are set on either side of the rows, about 2 ft apart, and black cotton is wound around them so that the row is caged with the cotton. As the plants grow, the tendrils seize the strands of cotton.

Straw or sedge peat is spread between the rows so that even if the plants of the taller varieties topple over under the weight of the crop, the pods are not mud-splashed or slug-damaged. Until the mulch is laid down, the soil between the rows is kept free of annual weeds by hoeing. Hand weeding may be done when the pea plants are small but I do not advise you to pull out large weeds later on. You will almost certainly loosen the roots of the peas and possibly pull up several of the plants.

Brussels sprouts and winter cabbage or broccoli may be set out between rows of dwarf peas in early June. The brassica plants will not need much room until some time after your peas have been eaten and the bine added to the compost heap.

If you do not mulch, remember that the more often you use the hoe between the rows, the more soil moisture you are likely to lose. In a dry season this may mean that even the row of the earliest variety may have to be watered. If short of water, the pods fail to swell and the plants and pods may suffer from mildew.

Harvesting. Do pick your peas before the pods are drumtight. At that stage they are old and lack flavour and sugar.

Varieties. (The average height is shown in inches):
First Early – Histon Mini (15), Forward (24), Early Onward (24), Dobie's Topcrop (30).

Second Early – Sutton's Chieftain (30), Onward (30), Histon Kingsize (40).

Maincrop – Alderman (60), Histon Maincrop (30).

Broad Beans

Broad beans are liked by some and disliked intensely by others. If you fall into the last group perhaps your dislike arises from your having been served broad beans with a skin like tough leather. I suggest you grow your own and pick the pods when the seeds in them are still swelling. After boiling the beans (not the pods!) ask the cook to drain and then to add a little butter, salt and pepper – delicious!

These very hardy beans are of two types – Longpods and Windsors. The Longpods are not quite so hardy as the Windsors. The seeds may be white, green or red. A sowing of a long-podded variety may be made in November or January in the south. In the north, an early sowing may be made under cloches in February. Sow seeds of Windsors in early April. Make a flat-bottomed trench as for peas, but a little deeper – say 3 in, allowing 9 in between each seed in a double row.

The plants come into bearing between mid-June to early July. If the plants tend to topple over, give them some support. Brushwood is ideal.

Broad bean plants attract the black bean aphis which, if not checked, can ruin the plants and the crop. Spraying with pyrethrum in May helps to ward off visits from the egg-laying females. If you prefer to use nicotine, do remember that this is a dangerous poison, though the poison does not enter the plant.

Varieties. *Longpod* – Dobies' Rentpayer, Aquadulce Claudia.

Windsor – Giant White Windsor. For cloche growing, The Sutton is strongly recommended.

Dwarf Beans

Dwarf beans are also known as French or Bush beans. Very often, although not always, the plants come into bearing before runner beans. The plants crop for three or four weeks, so, if you wish to have dwarf beans from July until mid-September, sow twice – in late April or early May and in mid-June. If the seeds are sown in cold, wet soil, they will rot. Cloches come in handy for warming up the soil. Sow the seeds in a trench 2 in deep and straddle them 8 or 9 in apart. Allow $2\frac{1}{2}$ ft between rows.

Cultivation. Keep weeds down between the rows by hoeing until early June, when a straw mulch may be laid between the rows and around the plants. In very windy areas, some brush-wood should be pushed in here and there alongside the plants to prevent their being blown over. Although dwarf beans stand up to drought better than runner beans, watering may be necessary in a very dry summer. I make shallow trenches on either side of the rows. After filling the trenches with water, I mulch with straw to prevent evaporation.

Harvesting. Pick the pods regularly – not only because they are delicious when young and tender but by picking at least twice each week you encourage the plants to set more pods.

Varieties. Selected Canadian Wonder, Masterpiece, The Prince, Golden Butter.

Runner Beans

The runner bean is Britain's favourite vegetable. This puzzles foreigners who are even more astonished when they hear of British gardeners showing more interest in the length of the pods than in the cooking quality. As for the cook – she is not interested in length of pod, but she likes them straight. To have straight runner beans, the plants must be given supports.

Bean poles are generally preferred. Bamboo canes are ideal and, if stored under cover when not in use, they last for years. My own crop of runners, however, is generally harvested from plants climbing on my wire mesh garden fence. It is essential that the trellis or fence be sufficiently strong to support the weight of the plants in August when so many good crops of runners are blown down by gale-force winds.

Sowing. Runner bean plants thrive in a deep, rich soil. If super-long beans are desired, a special trench for the plants should be made during the winter. The trench should be 2 ft deep and filled with a good mixture of well-rotted manure and topsoil. Sprinkle a little lime on the surface after filling the trench.

For runner beans in mid-July, sow under glass in April, using either 3 in deep boxes in which the seeds are spaced 2 in apart, or else $3\frac{1}{2}$ in peat pots in which only one seed is sown. Transfer the young plants to their growing positions in the garden in late May and protect the rows with cloches. When lifting plants raised in boxes, try to keep some of the compost around the roots. Plant with the trowel.

Most gardeners are satisfied with a first picking of runners in early August. For this purpose, the seeds are sown straight into the open ground, but as, like dwarf beans, they are not hardy, you must wait until conditions are suitable. This may be early May in the south to later in that month in the north. Cloches come in handy for this sowing. Sow the seeds about 2 in deep and, if in a single row, 9 in apart.

Cultivation. Keep the plants free of weeds and, if you wish, you may mulch the rows in June. By late July, the plants will have reached the top of the 6 ft supports, so pinch out the growing points to prevent a mass of weak growth. If the plants are short of water – and they need a great deal – the flowers will fall without setting pods. At the same time, black bean aphids will build up on the plants and ruin them. So never let your runner plants get thirsty and watch out for aphids. Liquid pyrethrum controls an outbreak of bean aphis until ladybirds arrive in sufficient numbers to do the job for you.

Syringing with clean water at evenings during hot weather was once a religious practice among gardeners. It certainly washes off dust from cement and other factories, but whether syringing helps the flowers to set is a moot point.

Pick the beans regularly and the plants will continue to crop until the first autumn frost. Arrange for friends or neighbours to pick and enjoy your runners when you are on holiday.

Runners on the flat. I do not favour the growing of runner beans on the flat but, if you have no suitable supports, here is how to do it.

Sow the seeds in a double row as advised for dwarf beans. When the plants are 12 in high, pinch out the growing point. This causes the plants to branch. Pinch out the branching stems also when they are about 18 in long and keep on pinching out now and then. The plants quickly form low bushes. Kelvedon Marvel is a good variety to choose if you grow your runners in this way.

Hammond's Dwarf Scarlet is a self-stopping runner. Sow and cultivate as for dwarf beans.

Varieties. Red flowered – Streamline, Sutton's Achievement, As Long as Your Arm.

White flowered – Carter's White Monarch, White Wonder.

Some information on peas and beans for the connoisseur will be found in Chapter XIV.

CHAPTER VII

THE CABBAGE FAMILY

BRUSSELS SPROUTS — CABBAGE — CAULIFLOWER AND
CAULIFLOWER BROCCOLI — SPROUTING BROCCOLI
KALE — BRASSICA TROUBLES

GARDENERS refer to cabbages and their relatives as brassicas because this group of vegetables belongs to the botanical genus *Brassica*. For rotation purposes, we also have to bear in mind that turnips, swedes and kohlrabi are members of the same family. Brassicas need lime. If the soil is too acid for the plants, a filthy fungus, known as Club Root, invades it. More will be said about Club Root later.

Sowing. Plants of cabbages and their kin are raised on a special seed bed from which the young plants are moved to their growing positions when four or five true leaves have been made. Choose an open, unshaded site for the seed bed, fork the soil to a depth of 2 or 3 in and remove any weeds and weed roots you come across. If the soil is in good heart, simply rake the bed level and remove any clods or large stones. Then firm with the feet and rake again. Gardeners who are not too happy about the state of their soil for seed bed purposes, replace the top inch or so with John Innes Potting Compost. A thick layer of sifted garden compost spread over the bed and firmed well is an alternative which I can personally recommend. Make the seed drills 8 in apart and 1 in deep. Sow thinly and, after covering the seeds with fine soil or compost, firm again. Prevent chickweed and other annual weeds from smothering the seedlings by hoeing (using the onion hoe) or by hand weeding.

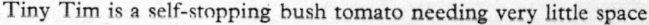

Dutch Net and Tiger melons ripening in the cold frame

Tiny Tim is a self-stopping bush tomato needing very little space

A cob of the new British hybrid Sweet Corn – Kelvedon Glory

Welsh onions are grown for salad use between February and June

Emerald Cross cabbages are compact and quick-growing

A vegetable marrow plant showing typical Cucumber Mosaic virus symptoms

BRASSICA SOWING TIMES

	Under cloches or in the cold frame	In the open	Transplant to growing positions
Brussels sprouts	March	April	June
Cabbage			
early summer	March	early April	May/June
summer, autumn, winter		mid-April	June
spring		July/August	September/October
Cauliflower			
early summer		August	Move plants to cold frame in October. Transplant in spring
summer	March	early April	June
autumn		mid-April	June
Cauliflower Broccoli, sprouting broccoli and kale		mid-April	June

Sowings under glass. Where, for the sake of earliness in cropping, the gardener makes use of glass protection, the seed bed is made in the way described above *but several weeks before the actual sowing date.* This is to allow the soil to warm up and, after the bed has been prepared, the light is set over the cold frame or the cloches stood over the row. The sun's rays will almost certainly dry out the protected soil so before sowing, flood the seed drills with water and sow in the mud left when the water seeps into the ground. Brassica plants are remarkably hardy and glass protection may be removed in early or mid-May.

Planting Brassicas. No brassica plant gives a good account of itself if the soil is unsuitable and although some cabbage varieties, sprouting broccoli and kale somehow manage to produce something on soils which are not up to scratch, cauliflowers and brussels sprouts are failures unless the soil is very fertile. The good gardener can assess the fertility of his soil by his results with these two crops and the new gardener may need quite a lot of patience whilst perfecting his soil so that it can produce sprouts and cauliflowers identical to those

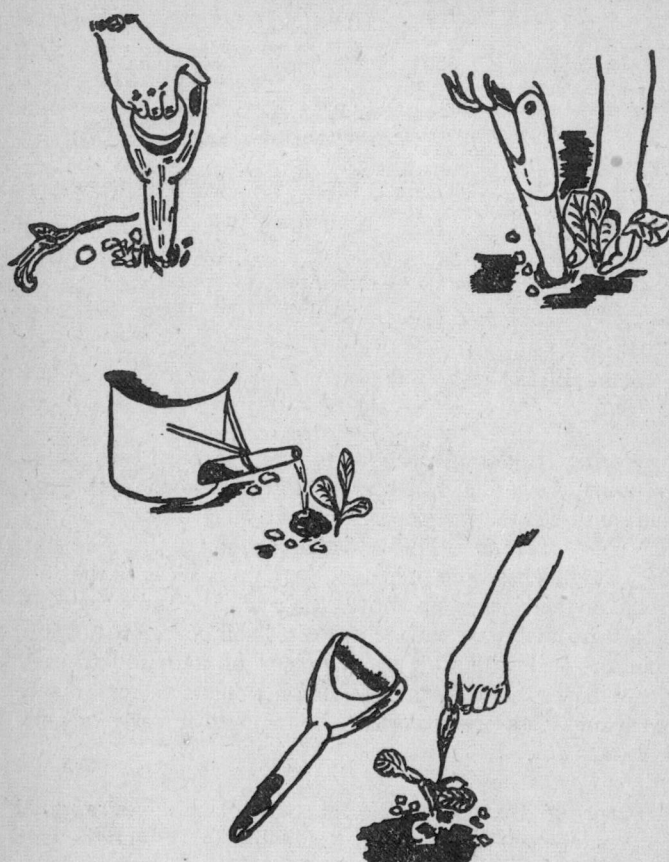

FIG. 3 Making planting holes with the cabbage dibber

featured on the seed packets. The regular manuring or composting and possibly liming of the soil will, in the end, give good results.

A loose soil cannot produce tight-hearted cabbages or firm sprouts, so where the site for brassica crops has been forked over in May to remove any weed growth, the soil must be firmed afterwards. Use your feet – wearing shoes or boots, of course – to do this. Mark the rows with the garden line and make the planting holes with the cabbage dibber, which is the top part of the handle of a spade or fork, with a pointed end.

If the soil is not really moist, fill the dibber holes with water. Wait until the water has drained away before planting. Plants of brussels sprouts, broccoli, cabbage and kale are set in the soil so that the lowest leaf is just at soil level. Cauliflower plants must not be planted so deeply. Push the dibber into the soil alongside the plants. This action will push soil against the roots and, at the same time, leave a handy hole for filling with water in dry weather. If the plants flag for a couple of days, do not worry. By the evening of the third day they will have recovered from the shock of being moved.

In dry weather, always drench the seed bed with water on the day before planting out. This will loosen the soil and allow the plants to be pulled out quite easily.

Planting distances. The amount of space each plant needs depends on the final size – which, of course, depends on the variety grown. The following measurements should be accepted as average.

	Between rows (inches)	Between plants (inches)
Brussels sprouts	30	30
Cabbage – spring, summer	15 to 18	12 to 15
autumn, winter	18 to 24	18
Cauliflower, cauliflower broccoli, sprouting broccoli, kale	24 to 30	18 to 24

General cultivation. After planting, brassica plants need very little attention. Hoeing will keep down weeds or, alternatively, the plants may be mulched with straw or peat. Planting between sheets of black polythene is another effective way of dealing with the weed problem. Although very closely related, the different types of brassicas have their own peculiarities. These will now be discussed.

Brussels Sprouts

The tasty sprouts are borne on the main stem of the plant and if the soil is not sufficiently firm and fertile, the sprouts will be very small and inclined to be loose. Plants from a March or April sowing start to bear usable sprouts from October if an early variety is chosen. A good many of us prefer to have sprouts somewhat later, especially around Christmas, and frost is credited with improving their flavour. Varieties like Irish Elegance, Thor (F.1. Hybrid) and Cambridge No. 3 are suggested. Sutton's Dwarf Gem is a short, compact variety of great use in the small garden but the sprouts form rather early in the autumn.

The formation of sprouts can be hastened by removing the growing point at the top of the plants in August or September. This is known as 'cocking'. The piece removed is about the size of a walnut. In windy areas, it is advisable to stake the plants in October and to draw some earth up around them, too.

Start picking sprouts from the bottom of the plants and harvest in batches as and when required. Finally, behead the plants and use the cabbage-like tops. Before adding the thick stems to the compost heap, slice them into small pieces with the spade.

Cabbage

Because there are special varieties for sowing at different times of the year, make sure that you sow the right ones at the right times. The following list will supply a family with cabbages all the year round, but few gardeners have room for all. Economically, the most valuable are those which mature in winter and late spring.

Variety	Sow	Plant out	Harvest
Sutton's April, Flower of Spring	late July/ early August	mid-September/ October	May to July
Primo, Sutton's June Star	March/ April	May/June	July/ September
Emerald Cross, Davington Middle Cross	mid-April	June	August/ October
Davington Late Cross	mid-April	June	October/ November
Christmas Drumhead, F.1 Hybrid Winter Monarch	mid-April	June	November/ December
January King	mid-April	June	January/ February
Savoy, Ormskirk Extra Late	mid-April	June	February
Winter White	mid-April	June	November

Spring cabbage. It is unfortunate that certain hardy varieties are termed 'spring cabbage' which they most certainly are not. Although the plants produce 'greens' for use in April, the tight heads are not ready for use until May or June. Sutton's April is possibly the earliest to mature and the small, tight cones are most welcome in May. Flower of Spring plants make gigantic cabbages for cutting in June. Seeds are sown on the prepared seed bed in late July or early August and the plants are moved to their growing positions in September or early October.

The site where early potatoes were grown that summer is ideal because the soil will contain dung or compost residues sufficient for the steady, but not rapid growth of the cabbage plants. In very cold areas, giving the plants cloche protection until early April is advisable. Where wood pigeons are a menace, the rows should be netted. Hoe between the plants in early November and again in March and April.

Summer and autumn supplies. The growing of summer and autumn cabbages calls for little comment. Providing the soil is well drained, firm and up to standard, round summer cabbages like Primo and Sutton's June Star give a good account of themselves. The new Davington cabbages are worth a trial. Seeds are offered by George Roberts of Faversham. Davington Middle Cross cabbages need plenty of room but the gardener with a sub-standard soil should not expect to cut magnificent heads, weighing around 12 lb, as I do in my garden. The flavour of these huge cabbages is excellent. Emerald Cross lacks flavour but is the ideal variety for the keen exhibitor. Christmas Drumhead is the general favourite for late autumn and early winter supplies, but other, newer introductions should also be tried.

Winter cabbage. January King cabbages vary quite a lot in size. If the plants are short of water in August or September, the cabbages are inclined to be somewhat small. The great blessing of this hardy variety is that the cabbages stand well without splitting. On the other hand, even specially selected strains are liable to produce a kind of large rosette of leaves instead of tight cabbages.

The hardy Savoy has distinctive, puckered leaves – in which caterpillars are very much at home! It is said that the savoy is rich in Vitamin C but I doubt whether much of the vitamin is available after boiling.

Winter White is quite new. The cabbages look rather like footballs. Cut them in November and store in nets hung from the ceiling of a dry shed, outhouse or garage. Tell your wife to slice the white cabbages very finely to save time in cooking.

Cauliflower and Cauliflower Broccoli

Both the cauliflower proper and the hardier cauliflower-broccoli are known botanically as *Brassica oleracea botrytis*. Claims are made that the summer cauliflower is more tender and tastier than cauliflower broccoli, but so far nobody has sponsored a national tasting test on the lines of some commercial television programmes!

It is an accepted fact that summer cauliflowers are more difficult to grow than the winter kinds (cauliflower broccoli). Quite often this difficulty could be overcome by ensuring that the plants are watered in a dry season. Neither the summer nor the winter cauliflowers do well if the soil is not in good heart and, because growth is quicker in summer than in winter, plants of summer cauliflowers need well manured or well composted ground.

For early summer cauliflowers, sow seeds of White King in the open in September. Move the seedlings to the cold frame in October, spacing them 4 in or so apart. Give water only when it is absolutely necessary and be prepared to lose a high percentage of the plants by late March, when they should be dug up carefully with the trowel and planted out at 18 in apart in their permanent quarters. Do not plant deeply. That is so very important with cauliflower plants. If you can give the plants cloche protection until late April, so much the better.

Summer and autumn cauliflowers. Sow seeds of Snowball or All the Year Round in the cold frame in March. If you have no cold frame, wait until the soil warms up in early April before sowing on a prepared seed bed outdoors. Transplant to their growing positions in May or June. Do not sow seeds of Boomerang, Sydney Market or South Pacific until mid-May. The snowy-white heads form in October and early November. These new cauliflowers from Australia may be rather on the late side for cold, northerly parts of the country. They do well here in the south.

Among the many cauliflower-broccoli varieties, there is none better than Reading Giant. Sow in April and set the plants in their growing position in June. The fine heads will not be ready for cutting until the following April. Yes, a year from sowing to harvesting is a long time to wait, but I can assure you they are worth waiting for.

The heads or curds of cauliflowers yellow with age or in bright sunlight. To prevent this, cut the heads as soon as they form. If several heads form at about the same time, break a large leaf over the curds.

Sprouting Broccoli

Here is a valuable spring crop which is easy to grow. On fertile, firm soil the plants are a yard across and a yard high and it pays to give them more room than the average distances suggested earlier on in this chapter. Make sure that you obtain seeds of Late White or Late Purple Sprouting and not those of early or Christmas sprouting. Sow in the seed bed in mid-April and transplant in June. Start picking or cutting the tasty shoots in March or early April and continue to harvest regularly until June.

There is also a little-known but tasty summer form, called calabrese.

Kale

The different kales – Scotch, Cottager's, Asparagus and Thousand Headed – are considered as the hardiest brassicas of all. Sow in the prepared seed bed in April and transplant to their permanent growing positions when the plants have made four or five leaves in June. On plants of Scotch kale it is the top which is the edible portion. This includes the growing point and fully developed leaves. The other kinds are grown for their side shoots in late winter and early spring. These are inclined to be on the bitter side unless picked when quite young.

Brassica Troubles

Club Root. This serious disease is caused by a fungus in the soil. Affected plants make little growth. When dug up, the roots of the plant are found to be badly swollen and may smell in a most unpleasant fashion if rot has started. Affected plants must be burnt. Liming the soil as part of the rotation of crops generally prevents Club Root. Souring of the soil by the too generous applications of organic or chemical fertilizers is one cause. A badly infected soil should not be used for brassicas for three years and should be limed each autumn.

Turnip Gall Weevil. Gardeners often confuse Turnip Gall Weevil swellings with Club Root. The galls or swellings made by the weevil grubs are either at or just below soil level. When the galls are cut, the maggot of the weevil will be found inside. Turnip Gall swellings are common and the small maggots do not appear to harm cabbages and other brassicas dealt with in this chapter.

Cabbage Root Fly. The female fly lays her eggs close to the plants in June. The maggots bore into the stem and the plants are dwarfed or may wilt and die. Firm planting in a firm, fertile soil prevents this trouble.

Caterpillars. Expect to see brown or green caterpillars gnawing your brassica plants from late June onwards. Derris dust will kill the caterpillars but, unless your plants are invaded, you may prefer to pick off the few caterpillars you come across. On healthy plants the damage is negligible.

Cabbage Aphis. Also known as Mealy Aphis. This is a serious trouble in some seasons. The aphids are greyish white and have a waxy appearance. A pesticide containing nicotine – such as Murphy Nicotine Dust – should be applied as soon as the trouble is noticed.

CHAPTER VIII

POTATOES

I SEE from my garden diaries that I have grown over 100 different varieties of potatoes. This will give you some idea of the many different varieties you will come across in seedsmen's catalogues.

There are three groups – First Early, Second Early and Maincrop. There is also a remarkable colour range. Not only are there potatoes with the skin colour one expects potatoes to have, but there are also kinds which produce tubers with golden, dark brown, red-mauve and purple-black skins. The embryo buds, called eyes, may be shallow or deep set, the skin of the potatoes may be very smooth or finely netted and you can have round oval or rather oddly shaped potatoes. There are varieties for boiling, chipping, for salads and for crisps!

Varieties

Let me try to help you choose suitable varieties to grow in your garden. If you have no room for them, omit Second Earlies and Maincrop. New First Early varieties continue to be bred but none, at the time of writing, is available to the gardener. Among established favourites Arran Pilot always crops well with me. Duke of York and Sharpe's Express are two other good varieties. Although many gardeners like Epicure, I do not find it a good cropper. First Earlies are ready for lifting in June and July. A Second Early needs more time to swell the tubers and the crops are heavier. Arran Banner is well liked but many gardeners do not plant Second Earlies at all. Instead, they grow an extra few rows of a First Early.

King Edward and Majestic are probably the best known maincrop varieties – very good they are, too. The new Pentland Crown is worth a trial. For chips, I like Aura and Kerebel. If you and the family enjoy a potato salad, I suggest Fir Apple from Sutton's of Reading.

Seed potatoes. Potato plants are raised from old tubers. Those on offer at your local garden shop or elsewhere have been grown in parts of Britain where greenflies find life rather difficult. Greenflies transmit weakening virus diseases from plant to plant. Because there are few greenflies where the potatoes are grown, the plants are seldom affected by virus troubles. Ministry of Agriculture officials visit the fields and issue certificates covering the health of the crop, which is lifted and sold as certified seed. In most parts of the country, it is wiser and safer to buy certified seed potatoes each season.

When the tubers arrive, take them out of the sack as soon as you can and set them in trays – Dutch trays from the greengrocer are ideal for the purpose. Stand the potatoes in the tray so that the end showing most eyes is uppermost. Stand the trays in an airy, light, frost-proof spot and, by late March or early April, each tuber will have made several strong, short sprouts.

Planting

Good Friday is the traditional day for potato planting. If you live in Cornwall, you may find other gardeners starting to plant in February and I suggest you follow suit. Good Friday sometimes falls in late March and, for many of us, conditions for planting are better in mid-April.

Potatoes do best on a well-drained soil which, at the same time, retains sufficient moisture so that the tubers swell well. Neither a chalky nor a heavy clay soil are suitable but both may be improved by heavy dressings of strawy manure or garden compost. The site for the potato crop is always manured or composted during winter digging, but never limed. This is because the plants favour a somewhat acid soil.

FIG. 4 Set seed potatoes in trays – eyes uppermost

First early potatoes need 12 in of row space with the rows 2 ft apart. Second Earlies and Maincrops make more top growth, so give the plants more room – 15 in between plants, 30 in between rows. Mark the rows with the garden line and take out trenches, using the spade or the draw hoe. The trenches should be 6 in deep on light soils and 4 in on others.

Discard any sick-looking tubers and any which have not sprouted well. Plant the healthy potatoes at the correct distances apart and with the shoots pointing upwards. Fill in the trenches, taking care that you do not knock off the tender shoots.

If there is the chance of a frost in May, draw some earth over the shoots poking through the soil. A severe frost blackens potato plants which, although they recover, are weakened.

Hoe between the rows to keep down weeds and, when the plants are 9 in or so high, use the draw hoe to pull up soil

FIG. 5 Using the draw hoe to earth up potato plants

around them. This practice is called earthing up. Some gardeners earth up twice. Whether earthing up is necessary is a debatable point and one which many orthodox gardeners are not very sure about.

If your soil is sandy, there is no need to make special trenches at planting time. Instead, you may use a potato dibber. This is not advised for other types of soil. Should you like to try two less orthodox methods, here are the details. Both obviate the need for earthing up. One is to plant the tubers in trenches (or use the potato dibber), keep down weeds until June and then mulch the bed with garden compost or straw.

Because it makes potato growing so easy, the black plastic method is becoming popular. Yard-wide polythene sheeting is used. Here is how to use it.

Examine the soil beforehand. If it has been compacted by winter rain, fork it to a depth of about 6 in and then rake level, removing any flints or large stones.

Now make two parallel rows of slits in the soil, 2 ft apart, with the spade. Midway between the slits, use the trowel to take out a row of 6 in deep planting holes. Set a sprouted potato tuber in each hole and cover with soil.

Then tuck one end of the roll of plastic into slits made in the ground at one end of the row and unroll the sheeting, tucking the edges into the parallel rows of slits on either side of you. When you reach the other end of the row, cut the sheeting and tuck the end into another slit in the soil. The purpose of the slits is to prevent the polythene from being blown off. Plant the next row in a similar fashion, leaving a gap of about 4 in between the plastic sheets.

In May, the potato shoots will make bumps beneath the plastic sheeting. Cut small holes with the scissors and pull the shoots through. No further cultivation is necessary.

Harvesting

First Earlies are lifted as soon as the tubers are of usable size and when the haulm is still green. When roots of Second Earlies are being dug in late summer and early autumn, the foliage may still be alive. Maincrop and plants of any other

FIG. 6 Potatoes in black plastic. Make planting holes
with the trowel. In May, pull shoots through slits made
with scissors

varieties are not left in the ground after October. During that month or possibly in September, the haulm will die.

Choose a sunny, dry day for harvesting. When digging out potatoes, push the fork tines deeply and at a vertical angle into the soil to prevent your spearing the tubers. Leave the potatoes on top of the soil for an hour or so after lifting so that they are quite dry before storing. Store in boxes or trays in a dry, cool but frost-proof place. Drape black polythene sheeting over the trays to prevent the potatoes from greening. Potatoes which green are not edible.

Pests and Diseases

Here are the main troubles you are likely to meet, although I trust you will not do so.

Dry Rot. Potatoes in sprouting trays shrivel and rot. Discard any which are affected.

Soil Pests. Cutworms, wireworms, leatherjackets, millipedes are more likely to attack potatoes grown on ground recently taken over for cultivation. Kill any you come across when digging and hoeing. Good, regular cultivation of the soil is the best control.

Slugs. Use a proprietary slug bait if the attack warrants it.

Potato Blackleg. Plants are dwarfed with very pale foliage and the base of the stems is brownish-black and shows rot. Lift and burn all affected plants.

Potato Root Eelworm. Like Blackleg, the infection probably arrives in your garden on the seed potatoes. Affected plants are short and weak and the leaves yellow and turn brown. The crop of potatoes is small as are the tubers. Potatoes should not be grown for several years on eelworm-infested soil.

Common Scab. Caused by a fungus which makes rough, brown scabs on the skin of potatoes. The flesh of the potatoes is not affected. Practising rotation and adding plenty of organic matter to the soil helps prevent this trouble.

Potato Blight. The fungus thrives in wet seasons. Small brown or black spots show on the leaves. The spots get larger and the plants collapse. In the meantime, the spores fall on to the soil and reach the potatoes which, when lifted, are often just an evil-smelling, pulpy mess. This very serious disease begins its attack in late June in the south-western counties, spreads over most of England in early July and reaches the north-east and Scotland in the middle of the month. Like many other fungus troubles, there is no cure but it can be prevented by spraying with a liquid copper fungicide such as Bordeaux Mixture. Fortunately for most of us, Potato Blight causes little, if any, damage, but it could!

CHAPTER IX

ROOT CROPS

THE ideal soil for root vegetables is one in which they may delve deeply and make shapely specimens like those featured on the seed packet. This means that if your garden soil is stiff clay or gravel peppered with flints, you cannot expect to grow first-class root crops until the soil has been cultivated for a few years. During those years you will improve the physical condition of the soil and this may entail some deep digging. Shorter-rooted varieties, called intermediates, should be grown in soils which are not favourable to long-rooted kinds.

Never sow seeds of root crops on land which has been recently manured. If you do, most of the roots will be misshapen.

Carrots

Carrot varieties are divided into two groups. The early maturing kinds make small, delicious roots for summer use. Maincrop carrots are dug up and stored in October.

The summer crop. For earliest results sow seeds of such varieties as Early Scarlet Horn, Early Nantes or Amsterdam Forcing in frames or under cloches in March.

The actual sowing time depends on the temperature of the soil. Pre-warm the soil by putting the frame light in position a week or so before you intend to sow or cover the site of the row with cloches. Use the rake to break down clods and remove all large stones when doing this. Make 1 in deep seed drills 6 in apart and, if you have the time and the patience, space the seeds ½ in apart. If you are like me, you will mix the seeds with some fine, dry sand and you will sprinkle the mixture along the rows as thinly as possible. Cover the seeds with soil and firm gently with your hands or your boots. Make sure that the cloche ends are fixed securely. If they flap open, the cloched row becomes a cold, windy tunnel.

Prevent seedlings of annual weeds from smothering the tiny carrot plants by frequent hoeings. Thin out the carrot seedlings when they are an inch or so tall, allowing each plant about an inch of row space. Pull for use when the carrots are sufficiently large.

In default of cloches or frames, the same varieties may be sown direct outdoors in April or May.

Maincrop. Popular maincrop varieties include St. Valery and James's Scarlet Intermediate. Egmont Gold is a new, good carrot to try. Wait until late April or early May before sowing the seeds, very thinly, in 1 in deep drills, a foot apart. Hoe regularly to keep down weeds. In July, pull out lots of the immature carrots for use in salads or stews, leaving one strong plant at every 4 in or 6 in in the rows.

The thinning operation is carried out over several weeks and the odour of freshly-pulled carrots may lead to an unwelcome visitor—the female carrot fly. She will be on the look-out for suitable spots for egg laying. Prevent her arrival by taking great care that leaves are not broken and that unwanted, small thinnings are buried inside the compost heap and not left around the garden. Firm soil also deters the carrot fly. I find it pays to water the rows after thinning carrots. Either by good luck or by taking the precautions I have suggested, my carrots have never been subject to carrot fly attacks.

In my garden, all cultivation ceases in July when I mulch the rows with sedge peat.

Harvesting. Choose a dry day for digging up maincrop

carrots. Set aside any you may have speared with the fork. Damaged carrots rot quickly so should be used at once. Store the crop in a pit or in boxes lined with damp sand. Lay the carrots in sandwich fashion between layers of moist sand. Store boxes in a cool place such as an outhouse or garage.

Troubles. In a weed-infested garden there is every chance that carrots will be ruined by wireworms and millipedes. Further information regarding these pests is given in Part 3.

Splitting of the roots may occur if the weather is very dry in July or August and if heavy rains follow the drought. It pays, therefore, to water the rows in a really dry season. Where aphids congregate on the crowns, a shortage of soil moisture should be suspected. Maybe near-by trees are stealing soil moisture.

Beetroot

In northern gardens cloches come in handy for the production of beetroot for early summer salads. I suggest sowing under cloches in late March, as one may do in the south and Midlands, too. In the south, a sowing may be made in the open in April – early May elsewhere.

If you sow under cloches, follow my suggestions regarding early carrots but leave 8 in between the rows. In the open, space the rows 12 in apart. Beetroot seeds are really clusters of several seeds and it is not difficult to sow three of them at 8 in stations along the row.

Except for hoeing and thinning when the plants are quite small, the growing of beetroot is not difficult.

Harvesting. Beet for summer salads are pulled as soon as they are large enough during July; more are pulled when required in August and September. Roots for storing are lifted in October. *Twist* off the foliage; do not cut it, because this causes bleeding. Rub off any dry soil adhering to them before

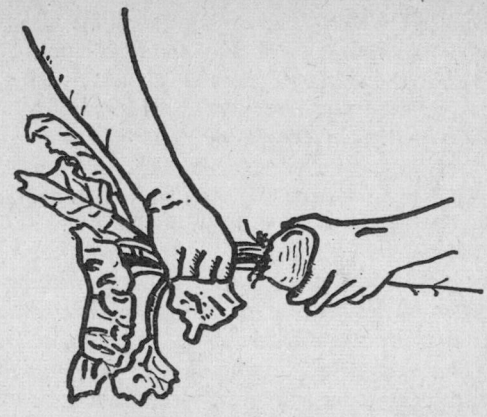

FIG. 7 Twist off beetroot foliage; do not cut

storing the beet, sandwich fashion, in dry ashes or dry peat in boxes.

Varieties. For summer salads: Crimson Globe Improved, Housewives' Choice.

For storing: Cheltenham Green Top, Dobies' Purple, Unwin's Intermediate.

Parsnips

Parsnips (if you like them) are a fine standby in February when there is often little else in the garden.

February is often mentioned as a good time to sow them, but it seldom is. I suggest that early April is better because germination is quicker in the warmer soil that month. Sow as for maincrop carrots and, to prevent the seeds from being blown across the garden fence, hold the packet close to the ground and sow thinly.

Hoe between the rows as soon as the seedlings show and use the hoe once or twice more before the final thinning. I thin twice – when the seedlings are small to about an inch apart and to 8 in apart in late June. The rows are then mulched with peat or straw. No more cultivation is needed.

Hard frost increases the sugar content and the flavour of parsnips, so I suggest that, like me, you wait until December before you consider starting to lift roots for use.

Canker is about the only trouble likely to be met in parsnips. The disorder causes patches of brown on the roots. In bad cases, rotting also occurs. Earthing-up the plants in August has been suggested as a preventive. I feel that mulching the plants with peat is also a good preventive measure. The varieties Avonresister and Tender and True show some resistance to canker.

Varieties. Tender and True, Improved Hollow Crown, Avonresister.

Turnips

Sow turnip seeds at any time during April and May in rows spaced a foot apart. Sow thinly in 1 in deep drills and thin the seedlings to 6 in apart when they are still quite small. The plants will not make good roots if thinning of the seedlings is delayed. In a dry season, give the plants a good soaking now and then. Popular varieties are Early Snowball and White Milan.

Cloches are useful for an early crop of turnips in June. Sow in late March and if you leave no more than 6 in or 8 in between the rows, you can house two rows under barn cloches. Thin the seedlings early and pay particular attention to watering when necessary. Remove the glass protection in late April.

The leaves of turnips (known as 'turnip tops') make excellent eating in spring. After all, this brassica is more or less a cabbage with a swollen root. For this purpose, sow seeds of

Hardy Green Round quite thickly in late July or early August. In colder areas the plants may need cloche protection during the winter. When harvesting, do not pull all of the leaves from any one plant. Take one or two from each so that the plants continue to make more foliage.

Swedes

Wait until early June before sowing seeds of Purple Top Improved in 1 in deep drills, 18 in apart. Thin the seedlings to 12 in. When hoeing, take care not to damage the roots. Swedes are hardy and are lifted as and when required from autumn until Christmas. Any not used by then should be dug and stored as suggested for carrots.

Turnips and swedes are members of the brassica tribe, so where possible, fit them into the cabbage rotation. They are also liable to some of the troubles met with in cabbage growing.

You will find radishes in Chapter XI and some other root vegetables in Chapter XIV.

CHAPTER X

THE ONION AND ITS RELATIVES

ONIONS prefer a medium loam or a reasonably light soil, providing such a soil does not dry out when the plants are bulbing up. There are three ways of producing good crops of onions for storing. Here is the easiest.

Onions from Sets

'Sets' are simply very small onions grown under crowded conditions the previous season by specialist seedsmen. The crop of tiny bulbs is dug and dried and offered for sale during the winter. For home use, if not for exhibition, their use is recommended.

Do not leave the onion sets to sweat in the bag after purchase. Spread them out in a tray and leave the tray in a cool room until late March.

The bed should be fertile, but not over-rich. Never grow sets on a bed which has been over-fertilized with strong organic or inorganic manures or fertilizers and never attempt to feed onion plants from sets with liquid manure. Where this is done, there is every likelihood of bolting. Bolting leads to unwanted seed heads and no onions for storing!

The bed will have been dug during the winter and at planting time in late March or early April will almost certainly need raking. Mark the rows at a foot apart and, providing the soil is reasonably loose, all that has to be done is to press the sets into it at 9 in apart. Alternatively, make shallow drills and bury the sets so that their tips just show above ground. Except for keeping the rows free of weeds, no special cultivation is necessary until around harvest time.

Use the spade to make slits into which black polythene sheeting is to be tucked

Unroll the sheeting and tuck it into the slits made with the spade

One of the author's compost heaps being covered with a large sheet of black polythene

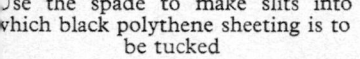

Salsify – one of the less usual root crops mentioned in
Chapter XIV

Aubergines are best grown in the greenhouse

The new parsnip Avonresister shows resistance to canker

However small the kitchen garden, aim at producing regular
supplies of salad crops

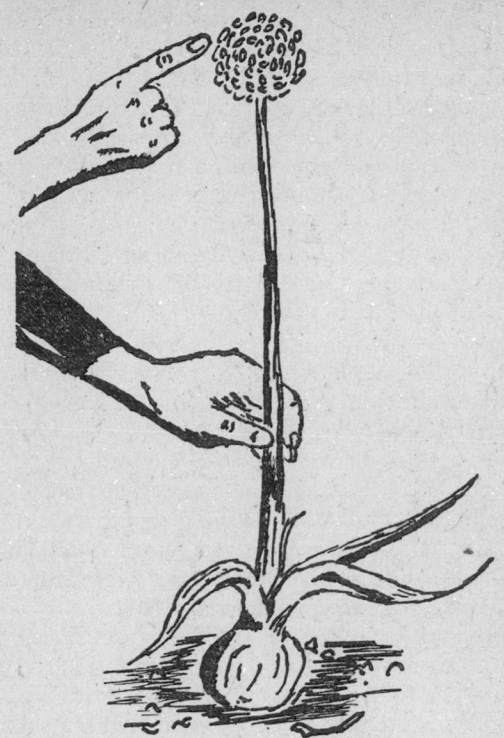

FIG. 8 An onion run to seed

Onions from Seed

Gardeners who prefer to raise their maincrop onions from seeds may sow in August or in March. Sowing in August is advisable if the onion fly is a serious pest in the locality.

August sowing. Sow quite thickly in 1 in drills. Hoe between the grass-like seedlings in October and, in cold areas, it pays to give the row cloche protection during the winter. Alternatively, sow in the cold frame if it is vacant in August.

K.G.—4

In early March, dig up all of the small onion plants and transplant them in a plot which has not been dug or forked for a month or more. If the soil has been disturbed, firm it well before planting. Although, according to the rotation plan in Part 1, onions fall into the 'other vegetables' section, if you were able to manure or compost the patch reserved for onions, so much the better. If you had no manure or compost apply a complete fertilizer at planting time.

Do not plant deeply. The planting distances suggested for onion sets are suitable. Giant Zittau and Sutton's A.1 are two good varieties for August sowings.

Spring sowing. Among the many varieties for sowing in spring, James's Keeping and Bedfordshire Champion come to mind. Selected Ailsa Craig certainly makes monster bulbs, but I have a feeling that they do not store too well.

Here again, a really fertile soil is very desirable. Sow in shallow drills, a foot apart, in March. Prevent weed growth by hoeing and start to thin in June and continue thinning until mid-July, so that finally one strong plant is left to grow at every 9 in in the rows. Use the thinnings in salads.

Take precautions to prevent an attack from female Onion Flies. Firm after thinning and never leave small thinnings around. Try not to break the foliage when cultivating, too.

A mulch after the final thinning saves further hoeing. You may, if you wish, feed the swelling bulbs in July and August. I suggest a weekly feed of liquid manure (see Chapter III). Great care must be taken to prevent sappy, weak growth. Too much feeding may lead to bolting or to disease.

Harvesting. Expect to see the first signs of ripeness in August. The foliage begins to yellow and should fall naturally to the ground. Stop all watering and feeding and, where the leaves on a plant here and there do not topple naturally, bend them soil-wards yourself.

When the foliage is quite dead and brittle, lift the onions on a dry, sunny day. Continue the ripening process by spreading the bulbs somewhere in full sun. In a wet season, dry off the onion crop on the greenhouse staging, in the conservatory or under cloches.

When the bulbs are quite dry, rub off any dead roots, dry soil and very loose scales and store in trays or, better still, rope them. The diagrams show how to do this.

Spring onions for salads. As has been mentioned, the thinnings of maincrop onions, raised from seeds sown in spring, provide 'spring onions' for the summer salad bowl. Where maincrop onions are raised from seed sown in August or from sets, there will be no suitable thinnings for salad use. White Lisbon is the variety specially grown for salad onions. The seeds may be sown in August or March. Sow quite thickly and start pulling the onions as soon as they are of suitable size for use.

Never leave the bulbs to get large unless you like spring onions which are as hot as mustard.

Shallots are generally grown for pickling, although they may also be used in the kitchen to replace onions. This is a very easy crop to grow. Buy 1 lb shallots and push them into the soil during March. Space the bulbs 9 in apart with 12 in between rows. Except for weeding, no cultivation is necessary. Lift the clumps in July, dry as onions and store in a cool place.

If you prefer to grow a pickling onion, sow seeds of Small Paris Silver-Skin in early April. Sow fairly thickly on poor soil and harvest the crop in July. Do not thin the plants at all.

Tree onions are the only onions you can harvest when the ground is under several feet of snow. The plants bear clusters of small bulbs on top of the 3 ft to 5 ft shoots. The plants take from two to three years to come into bearing and need some form of supports to prevent their toppling over.

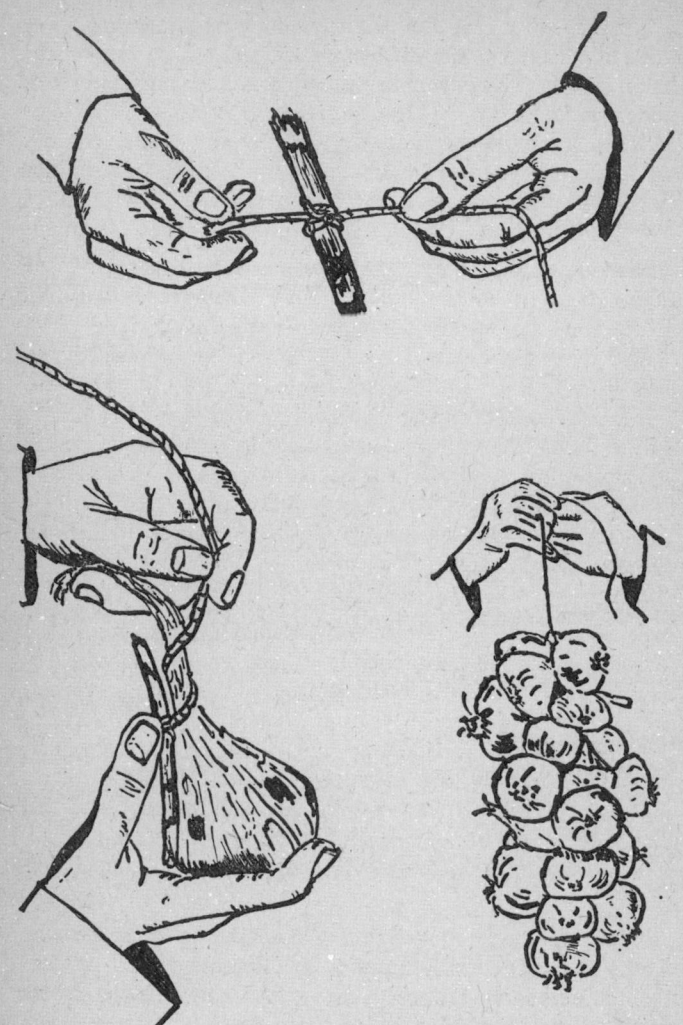

FIG. 9 Tie a short piece of wood at one end of the rope

The Welsh onion forms clusters of spring onions. Dig up the clump at any time in the late winter and spring months, take what you want and replant a cluster of two or three to maintain the succession for the following season.

Pests and diseases. I am happy to record that my own onion crops have never suffered from pests and diseases and I hope you have similar good fortune. Apart from Onion Fly maggots and perhaps wireworms, insect pests should not be troublesome. Stem and Bulb Eelworm and Onion White Rot both cause the bulbs to rot. There is no cure, so lift and burn all affected onions and do not attempt to grow members of the onion family on or near the site for several years. Rotating the onion bed around the garden over the years prevents a build-up of pests.

Leeks

If you live north of the Mersey, I think you may well get better advice on leek growing at the local than from any book by a Kentishman! Not that we southerners do not like leeks – we do – but we certainly do not make much fuss of them. Here is the Kentish way of growing them.

The seeds are sown fairly thinly in the seed bed in March or April. The seedlings are dug in June and transplanted to a reasonably fertile bed. Rows, 12 in apart, are marked by the garden line and holes are made, 8 in apart, with the cabbage dibber along the rows. One plant is dropped into each hole and the holes are then filled with water. Except for weeding now and then, no cultivation is normally carried out.

I find it helpful to soak the bed with water in late July and to apply a mulch. This may be sedge peat, straw or even raw sawdust. Dig the leeks when required during the winter. Leeks seldom suffer from pests and diseases.

The Lyon is popular in the south; Musselburgh in the north. I like Marble Pillar.

For garlic, see Chapter XIV.

CHAPTER XI

THE SALAD BOWL

LETTUCE – RADISH – CUCUMBERS
MUSTARD AND CRESS

FRESH salads are an important part of the diet and those we grow are certainly fresher than those at the shop . . . and in salads, freshness is all.

Lettuce

The foundation of spring, summer and autumn salads is lettuce. There are the soft butterheads, the crispheads and cos. All of these form tight hearts. Butterheads and crispheads are known as cabbage lettuce. Cos lettuces are tall and the leaves are smooth. Salad Bowl is a loose-leaf variety in which the whole plant is not cut but the leaves are pulled as and when required. The great thing with lettuces is to have a constant supply for as many months as possible and the table below shows how this may be done from late May until early winter.

Sow	Transplant	Variety
March (under cloches or in the cold frame)	Thinnings in April	May Queen (also known as May King)
April	late May or early June	Unrivalled (Sutton's) (White-seeded) Peson, Giant White Cos (Dobie's), Salad Bowl
May to late July	in succession	Peson, Windemere

For very small spaces and small families, Tom Thumb is an excellent little lettuce for successional sowing from March onwards.

Early summer supplies. Weather conditions may allow you to sow in February in some seasons. This can be done by the use of frames or cloches.

Pre-warm the bed in the cold frame or the row to be cloched by setting the glass in position a fortnight before sowing. Prepare the seed bed as for cabbage (see page 48) and leave 9 in between rows. The onion hoe is handy for making the seed drills. Sow thinly and, after germination, water now and then if the bed dries somewhat.

About a month after sowing, thin the seedlings to 8 in apart. Dig up some of the excess seedlings and plant them beneath another row of cloches or, if weather permits, in the open.

FIG. 10 The onion hoe is handy for making seed drills under cloches or in the frame

Remove the cloches or open the frame light in May. The first lettuces will be fit to cut in late May or early June.

These early lettuces may be treated as a catch crop on ground planned for summer crops like tomatoes, cucumbers and vegetable marrows.

Summer lettuces. Sow outdoors on a well prepared seed bed (or in a seed box) in mid-April. Transplant the seedlings to their growing positions when of sufficient size to handle. Plant in rows a foot apart, not deeply. Allow each plant 8 in of row space. Catch and successional cropping may be practised by growing the summer lettuces where plants of winter cabbage and broccoli are to be set out alongside the lettuces in June. You will have cut and eaten all of the lettuces before the brassicas need all available space.

Aim at a continuous supply of lettuce right through to September at least. To achieve this, sow again in April and in May. From then onwards, however, instead of sowing in a seed bed and then transplanting, sow the seed direct into the growing position, sparsely and in very shallow drills. Thin out the seedlings when they are quite small and hoe or mulch to keep down weeds. Water, too, in dry spells. Sedge peat is a first-class mulching material for lettuces.

Although a self-hearting variety, plants of Dobie's Giant White Cos form finer hearts if the leaves are tied rather loosely together in late June or early July.

Autumn lettuces. To have lettuces in November and December is chancy but worth trying. Sow Sutton's Unrivalled in early August, thin the seedlings later that month and cloche the row when colder weather starts in September. If you are fortunate, you will cut rather loose lettuces during November and possibly on Christmas Day.

Radish

Rapid growth and sufficient food, water and space are the secrets of success with radishes. Sow seeds of Sutton's Red Forcing alongside or in the same cloched bed as early summer lettuce. Thin the seedlings when they are small to leave each with 1 in of space on all sides. Sow on and off in small batches outdoors from early or mid-April until late July. Good varieties are French Breakfast (red, tipped white), Scarlet Globe (red) and Icicle (white).

Autumn and winter radish. Sow in late June and sow very thinly because the large plants have to be thinned to 9 in apart.

Black Spanish, China Rose and Japanese All Season are the varieties to choose. Dig the roots when required during September and October. Those remaining should then be stored in a pit of moist sand outdoors. Although these radishes are big, they are not hot. Serve them grated in salads or sandwiches.

Cucumbers

There are two kinds of hardy cucumber and, in colder areas where the plants need frame or cloche protection, only varieties which may be grown without a trellis should be chosen. King of the Ridge and Bedfordshire Prize Ridge are popular. The new American Burpee F.1 Hybrid may be grown on the flat or on a trellis. The Japanese cucumbers recently introduced by Thompson & Morgan and by George Roberts need tall supports. Whichever variety is chosen, economy of space demands that only a few plants should be raised, for the average family seldom needs more than one cucumber at a time. Greenhouse cucumbers are dealt with in Chapter XVI.

For an early crop. Sow two or three seeds in $3\frac{1}{2}$ in peat pots filled with a suitable compost in late April or early May. Stand the pots in the cold frame or under a cloche and water now and then with a fine rose to prevent drying out. Pinch out the weaker seedlings and transplant the strong ones in early June 24 in apart under cloches or in the cold frame, without removing them from the peat pots. An outdoor bed may be a yard wide with 18 in between the plants.

Although the plants do not need the heavy dressings of organic manure which greenhouse kinds need, growth is more rapid and the cucumbers more succulent if some well-rotted manure or garden compost is spread over the bed just before planting out. Prevent stem rot by leaving almost an inch of the peat pot above soil level. Tear off any dry pieces of the pots. If the soil is not wet, fill the planting holes with water before planting, but do not plant until the water has drained away.

When the plants have made seven leaves, pinch out the growing point to encourage branching. Weed when necessary and give water if the soil appears dry. To prevent the plants from being splashed, apply the water directly to the roots via a clay pot sunk in the soil alongside the plants. See Fig. 12(b) on page 98. A straw mulch smothers weed seedlings and also helps prevent slug damage to the cucumbers. Liquid manure feeds should be given from mid-July onwards.

Cut the cucumbers when they are of full size and before they show any yellowing. The more often you pick, the more cucumbers you may expect. Pollination is necessary so do not remove any flowers at all.

Outdoor sowing. In warmer parts of the country, the seeds may be sown direct outdoors in mid-May. Sow two or three seeds at each station on the prepared bed. To assist germination and to give protection to the seedlings, jam jars (open end downwards) may be used as miniature cloches. Reduce the seedlings to leave one at each station when they are forming their first true leaves. These are triangular and rough; the seed leaves are oval and smooth. Further cultivation is as already described.

Trellis cucumbers. The new Japanese varieties produce cucumbers which may be as long as those we associate with greenhouse-grown plants. Raise the plants from seeds sown in pots in April or May and set them 15 in apart on the prepared bed. The trellis should be 6 ft high. In Japan, this is a neat bamboo affair, but the plants grow equally well on a trellis of scrap iron poles linked together with steel wires. Tie the plants regularly to the supports. When the plants reach the top, pinch out the growing point. Except for weeding, mulching, watering and feeding there is nothing else to do but harvest the fine cucumbers.

Hardy cucumbers do not normally suffer from any pests or diseases. Even Cucumber Mosaic Virus is more common on vegetable marrows than on cucumbers. The symptoms are yellow streaks on the leaves accompanied by distortion of the leaves and the plants are dwarfed. Pull up and burn affected plants.

Mustard and Cress

Mustard and cress is a welcome addition to early spring salads. Fill a seed tray with bulb fibre, firm well and water with a fine rose. Sprinkle the seeds quite thickly on the surface of the fibre and stand the tray in a dark cupboard for about a week. By that time, long white stems will have been made and it is then time to move the box to a sunny window or to a warm greenhouse or conservatory, where the leaves will turn green.

Cress takes a little longer to grow than mustard so sow cress seeds three days before the mustard in a separate container. You may use the same bulb fibre for at least two sowings.

Other salad crops. Refer to the index for other salad crops – beetroot, celeriac, celery, chicory, chives, endive, greenhouse cucumbers, spring and Welsh onions, tomatoes.

CHAPTER XII

OUTDOOR TOMATOES

GROWING FROM SEED — PLANTING OUT
ROUTINE CULTIVATION — RIPENING-OFF AND
HARVESTING — VARIETIES — TOMATO TROUBLES

TOMATO growing is considered by many as a chancy business. It certainly is not at all chancy in the southern counties and, if you have failed with the crop, I hope you will try again after reading this chapter. You may be told that growing your own is rather foolish because, when you are picking your own ripe fruit, prices are low in the shop. In some summers, however, tomatoes are dearer than at Christmas. In my garden, the first tomatoes ripen in early August and it is with great regret that we eat and enjoy the last of them some time in October.

Growing from Seed

Gardeners who do not own a heated greenhouse generally buy young plants from a local shop or nursery in late May or early June but if you live in the south you may with great advantage raise your own by sowing seed in a cold frame or under cloches during the first two weeks of April. The advantages are that seeds are cheaper than plants, the plants will be raised in composts and soils free of serious fungoid pests, you will ensure that the plants are hardened off before being set out in the open and, above all, you may grow the variety you wish to. This last point is very important. Few if any nurserymen raise plants for sale of the new, hardy tomato, Outdoor Girl, and no nursery or shop sells plants of the delicious yellow tomatoes.

Those who live in the colder parts of the country had

perhaps better not attempt to raise their own seeds unless they have a heated frame or greenhouse.

Sowing. Fill 3½-in size peat pots with sifted garden compost or John Innes Potting mixture, water well and then press two or three seeds into the wet compost. Sprinkle a little dry compost on top to cover and water again, using a very fine rose. Using the trowel, make 1 in deep, flat-bottomed trenches in the bed of the frame or on the site to be cloched. Stand the pots closely together in these trenches and put on the frame light or cloches.

Thin the seedlings to leave one in each pot and, in mid-May, move the pots apart if the plants need more space. Pay particular attention to watering because the pots must on no account be allowed to get dry.

Before setting out the plants in the open, acclimatise them to outdoor conditions. Do this gradually. A week before the intended planting-out day, leave the light off the frame or take off the cloches during the daytime, but replace them in the evening. A couple of days before planting out, remove the glass entirely.

Planting Out

Tomato plants need all the sunshine and warmth possible in our cloudy summers. A first-class spot for them is just in front of a south-facing wall. The wall protects the plants from cold, north winds and the radiated heat from the wall hastens the ripening of the fruit. If you have no suitable wall site, choose the sunniest positions in the garden.

The soil should be firm and fertile. If the bed has been forked over recently, tread the soil to firm it and then rake it to leave it level and tidy. Well rotted farmyard manure or garden compost may be added as a mulch to the bed before or just after planting.

If the plants have been raised in peat pots, the roots will have passed through the pot wall into the bed below. Dig up the pots to prevent breaking these roots. Make the planting holes 15 in apart and leave 30 in between rows. Unless the soil is really wet, fill the planting holes with water. Wait until the water has drained away before planting. If the plants are in clay pots, invert the pot and tap smartly with the trowel handle. The plant should come out of the pot with the soil ball intact. Tear off mulch or polythene pots and the dry, top portion of peat pots. Do not plant deeply. Firm the soil around the plants after planting.

If you can give the rows cloche protection from planting out until late June or early July, so much the better.

Except for the self-stopping bush varieties – about which see later on in this chapter – tomato plants need supports. If you are growing no more than a couple of dozen plants, provide each of them with a stout bamboo cane. My own tomato plants are set alongside a 4 ft high trellis. This consists of several stout stakes linked together with three or four strands of wire.

If you are as keen on weedless gardening as I am, you may like to set the tomato plants between two sheets of black polythene. Anchor the sheeting to the soil by making slits with the spade as explained in the chapter on potatoes, but allow 30 in between the parallel rows and leave an 8 in gap between the sheets. Set the plants at 18 in apart in this narrow gap. Alternatively, lay down a straw mulch in early July.

Routine Cultivation

Unless the plants are growing in a mulch, hoe now and then to keep down weeds. Give ample water in dry spells and, if you consider that the plants would benefit from feeding, wait until the first tomatoes have started to swell before doing so. Home-made liquid manure is as good as any proprietary fertilizer.

Tie the plants to their supports each week from late June until early August. Use raffia or soft string and do not tie tightly. If you do, the ties may cut into the stems as they swell.

Pruning and stopping. One of the most important commandments for outdoor tomatoes is to restrict growth to the main stem only and to arrest all growth in early August. Examine the plants regularly and pinch out all side shoots arising at the base of the plants and those which form in the leaf axils – see Fig. 11. If you have not grown tomatoes before, study this diagram carefully, for, if you are not quite sure, you may make the mistake of pinching out the flowering shoots which form on the main stem.

FIG. 11 Pinching out the side shoots of tomatoes

Tomato plants are 'stopped' in early August by pinching out the growing point at the top of the plants just above the second leaf beyond the third or, in the few hot seasons we enjoy, beyond the fourth truss of flowers or small tomatoes. Shortly after 'stopping', the plants make quite a lot of new side shoots. These also should be nipped off. The idea is to concentrate the plants' energy on ripening a limited amount of fruit before cold weather sets in.

Self-stopping bush tomatoes. Raise the plants as suggested earlier in this chapter. When setting out the young plants in early June, allow 2 ft of space all ways. Tuck straw around and beneath the bushy plants in July or much of the fruit will flop to the ground and be spoilt. No supports are required and you have no pinching out or stopping to do.

Ripening-off and Harvesting

In a cool summer, the greater part of the crop will not ripen naturally outdoors and measures must be taken to induce it to do so. One method is to strip off all of the leaves in September, untie standard plants from their supports and lower the plants on to some clean, dry straw. Set cloches over the row and continue picking ripe tomatoes.

If you have no cloches, dig up the plants in September and hang them in the greenhouse. Alternatively, wait until late September and then pick off all of the fruits and store them in a drawer in a warm room. The very small green tomatoes on the top trusses may never ripen, but they make excellent chutney.

Varieties

Nearly all of the many varieties listed in the seedsmen's catalogues were bred for glasshouse cultivation, so be careful. The following are recommended for outdoor growing.

Outdoor Girl. This new variety is an early ripener and is by far the most suitable for outdoor growing. The crop is good, the flavour is generally liked and most of the tomatoes are even in shape.

Moneymaker. This heavy cropping variety is still the

favourite for outdoor cultivation. It is likely to be superseded by Outdoor Girl.

Golden Boy. Unfortunately this is not an early ripener, but the plants crop well in my own garden in Kent. The golden tomatoes weigh up to 1 lb each and the flavour is delicious.

The Amateur and **Golden Amateur.** Both are self-stopping bush varieties. I have picked as many as 10 lb of tomatoes from one plant of The Amateur in my garden.

Tomato Troubles

Tomatoes grown outdoors do not suffer from many pests but you are likely to meet with two very serious troubles. The first is Tomato Mosaic Virus, which results in hard, fern-like leaves and a poor crop. There is really nothing you can do to prevent or cure the trouble. Burning the infected plants is advisable.

Blight is a fungus which thrives in warm, wet weather. The symptoms are dark brown patches on both green and ripe tomatoes; the leaves and stems may also be affected. There is no cure but you can try to prevent the trouble by spraying the plants with Bordeaux mixture or a proprietary copper fungicide at fortnightly intervals from mid-July. Pull up and burn any infected plants. *The fruit cannot be eaten.* It sours and rots.

For tomato growing in the greenhouse, see Part 3.

CHAPTER XIII

OTHER VEGETABLES

Jerusalem Artichoke

THE Jerusalem artichoke has no connection with the Holy City. It comes from Canada, where it was discovered by French explorers 300 years ago. The word 'Jerusalem' is simply the British attempt at pronouncing the Italian 'girasole'. I understand that the artichoke is free of starch and low in calories. If you have health worries, ask your doctor if Jerusalem artichokes should replace potatoes in your diet. Only you yourself can decide if they are worth eating.

Plant the tubers anywhere in the garden in February where little else will grow – 6 in deep and a foot apart. No cultivation is necessary except for pulling out a few weeds. Dig the tubers in November and store as suggested for carrots (Chapter IX). The Jerusalem artichoke is closely related to the sunflower and the very tall plants make a useful windbreak in windy areas.

For the epicurean Globe Artichoke, see page 100.

Asparagus

Asparagus plants need a lot of space but, once planted, they may crop season after season for 30 years. The plants do best in rather light, sandy soils. Where the subsoil is clay, go down really deeply, mixing rubble and gritty material into it. The top spit must also have free drainage, so add sand and leaf mould to it if the soil is on the sticky side.

The alternative method of preparing an asparagus bed is to leave things alone down below and to prepare a bed a yard wide and raised up 12 in on top of the existing soil. Rich soil is not required. A good bed should consist of loam, leaf mould, sand

and a little lime. Such a bed will take two rows of plants 18 in apart in the rows. Order two-year-old roots from the best possible source, insisting that you require male plants only as these are more prolific than the berry-bearing females.

Planting is rather tricky, and do try to plant as soon as the roots arrive. Every hour counts. Take out a 9 in deep trench before the arrival of the plants and spread out the spider-like roots on a slight mound at the bottom of the trench. After covering the roots with soil, the crowns of the plants should be about 5 in below the bed level. Plant in April and cut *nothing* from the plants in the first season. Feed the bed each spring with an inch-thick mulch of well rotted manure or garden compost.

In the second and subsequent seasons, start cutting the succulent shoots when about 4 in high in May and stop cutting in mid-June. Sever the shoots well below soil level, using a sharp knife. Allow the plants to grow naturally throughout the summer and cut the stems down to the ground in late October.

Suggested varieties are Superior (Marshall's) and Sutton's Perfection.

Celery

There are three kinds of celery – blanched, self-blanching and green. Unless you are the kind of gardener who has beginner's luck, I do not advise you to grow celery until you have had a few years' practical experience with easier vegetables. You also need a good supply of manure for this crop.

Sowing. If you have a heated greenhouse, sow the seed of whichever of the above sorts you choose in trays or pots filled with John Innes Seed Compost in March. Harden off the plants in the cold frame before planting out in early June. Alternatively, buy a dozen plants in late May or early June. Celery is a very greedy feeder and the bed must be very rich. You must also be prepared to water regularly throughout the summer unless you live somewhere where there is generally a great deal of rain.

Self-blanching. This is useful for late summer salads and is easier to grow than the usual winter varieties which are dealt with later. One of the best places for this crop is in the cold frame. Add well rotted manure, garden compost or hop manure when preparing the bed and set the plants 9 in apart. Do not plant deeply but flood the bed with water afterwards. Keep the light closed for a few days, then prop up the light by about 2 in during the day and close at night to prevent possible frost damage.

Remove the light in mid- or late June and water often. Celery is a marsh plant and revels in a great deal of moisture. In a dry summer, if you fail to flood the bed weekly be prepared to see the plants bolt or produce stringy sticks fit only for soups. In mid-July, tuck straw around the plants to assist the blanching.

Lift the plants for use in late August and September.

American Green Celery. This is grown in the same way as Self Blanching. The celery is eaten green, so there is no need to worry about blanching at all and the plants may be grown in the open. Give cloche protection in early June if there is risk of a late spring frost.

Autumn and winter celery. Celery for autumn and winter use must be blanched. Set the plants at the bottom of a foot deep, 15 in wide, trench. The soil at the bottom of the trench should be replaced by a rich mixture of manure (if you have any), garden compost and lawn mowings. Drench this rich mixture with water and firm well when the water has drained away. All of the soil removed in making the trench should be banked neatly alongside it. You will not need it until August, so use it for lettuces or radish.

Set the celery plants in a double row so that each plant has

9 in of space on all sides. Remove weeds by hand and keep the bottom of the trench nicely moist.

Blanching is carried out in three stages. About mid-August is the time to start. Hold each plant tightly to prevent soil entering the heart and heap about 4 in of earth around all of the plants. Water well and, a fortnight later, earth up again, using the soil alongside the row. Two or three weeks later, tie the foliage of each plant together and earth up finally to just below the green leaves. Firm the banked up soil around the plants with the spade.

Start digging the blanched celery in November and continue lifting as and when you wish until February. I suggest you spread a little straw over the plants in November to protect them from severe frost and from snow.

Celery Fly maggots are a nuisance in some seasons. The eggs are laid on the leaves and the maggots tunnel into them. Watch out for them and squeeze the paper-like burrows with the maggots inside them. Dusting with soot now and then is believed to deter the female flies.

Varieties. Each seedsman seems to offer different varieties of celery and many of them may be no more than synonyms. The following appeared in the catalogues of reputable seedsmen should do well.

Self Blanching: Golden Self Blanching or Ryders Golden.

Green: American Green or Giant Pascal.

For blanching: Sutton's Unrivalled Pink, Solid Red, Selected Red or Dobie's Prizetaker White.

Rhubarb

The Cinderella of so many gardens and allotments is rhubarb. Just because it will grow under shocking conditions, it is unfair to treat it badly. Please do not think that I am trying to show off when I say that the best rhubarb bed I have seen so far is my own. Rhubarb deserves good treatment because it is such a valuable crop. Stewed rhubarb and cream is always welcome between April and August and sticks are also pulled for wine in June and again in September.

Choose an unshaded, open site for the rhubarb bed – one where the clumps may settle down peacefully for ten years. The plants cannot do well if shaded, if trees nearby steal the soil moisture or if the gardener periodically forks or hoes the soil around them.

Probably the earliest variety is Timperley Early. Mr. J. E. Marsland, Clay Lane Nurseries, Timperley, Cheshire, offers plants. Hawkes Champagne is a very popular variety, although the plants must be watched in May, when weakening seed heads are produced. These should be cut off as soon as noticed. Late rhubarb for jams and wines is not popular, but I grow the Canadian variety, MacDonald, solely for wine-making. I hope that roots of this very fine variety will be offered for sale here one day – soon.

Rhubarb stools are planted in the late autumn. The soil should have been cleaned of all weed roots and then manured or composted. Make the planting holes 4 ft apart and sufficiently large to take the roots. Plant firmly but take care not to bury the pink buds on the crowns. After planting, cover the bed with rotted farmyard manure or garden compost. A similar top dressing should be applied every second autumn if you are aiming at rhubarb as good as mine.

During the first season after planting you will have to pull out weeds here and there. In future years, the spreading leaves of the plants will inhibit weed growth. Do not pull a single stick of rhubarb in the first season. In the second season, do not over-pull. In subsequent seasons, pull often but *never* over-pull. That weakens the plants. When pulling sticks of rhubarb, grasp them as low down as possible so that they are not broken.

You are not likely to meet any pests and diseases.

The forcing of rhubarb in the greenhouse is covered in Chapter XVI.

Spinach

There are three main sorts of spinach: the Round-Seeded summer spinach, the Prickly or winter spinach and various pseudo-spinaches which to most palates are equally good. As in lettuces, peas and so on, the aim should be to keep up a continuous supply, particularly during the summer months, by successional sowings. The summer and winter varieties are short lived. Give both of these good, rich soil and copious watering in dry summer spells.

Of the summer spinaches it is best to choose a 'long standing' variety. Begin to sow the seed in mid-March and, if you are keen on this vitamin-rich crop, make successional sowings every fortnight until July. Sow in 1 in deep drills, spaced 1 ft apart, and thin the seedlings to 3 in as soon as you can and keep the plants supplied with water. Prickly-seeded varieties are sown in July or August.

Of the pseudo-spinaches, the most usual is Spinach Beet (or Beet Spinach). It is very long-lasting and a 20 ft row is enough for most people, whereas 30 ft may be needed for the fleeting Summer Spinach. Spinach Beet is reputed to stand up to drought better than Round Seeded spinach.

Another beet to provide good spinach-type leaves is Seakale Beet or Swiss Chard – as it is also known. The glossy white, thick midribs may be treated as seakale and the green, leafy part stripped and used as spinach.

Only a few leaves should be picked from any type of spinach at any one time. Never strip any one plant.

Vegetable Marrows and Pumpkins

No kitchen garden is complete without the vegetable marrow or, as American and Canadian gardeners say, 'summer squash'. There are two kinds of plants – bush and trailing. The older bush varieties were considered to be rather poor croppers. This does not hold good for new introductions.

Plants may be raised from seeds by sowing in the cold frame between mid-April and early May. Using peat pots, sow two seeds in each and remove the weaker plant when the first true leaves (triangular in shape) are forming. They must stay in the frame until the danger of late frosts has passed, which means early June, when they may be planted out.

Seeds may also be sown in mid-May where the plants are to grow. Sow two seeds at each station and, to hasten germination, stand a jam jar (open end downwards) over them. Do not sow more deeply than 1 in and pull out the weaker seedling if both germinate.

Once they get going, marrow plants are always hungry. In the old days the plants were often grown on a pile of rotted manure. How you enrich your marrow bed will depend on what you have to hand. I spread a generous layer of garden compost over the whole bed. How much space you will give each plant varies with varieties. A bush type plant needs $2\frac{1}{2}$ sq ft of surface area; a trailing kind needs a great deal more unless you train your plants by the space-saving methods suggested in Part 3. There is no need at all to pinch out or stop plants of the trailing varieties.

The plants bear separate male and female flowers and you will have no marrows unless the female flowers are pollinated. Bees, flies and ants generally transfer ripe male pollen grains to the female flowers, but they sometimes fail in their duty and it is best to make sure by hand pollination. This is quite easy. Pick off a male flower during the morning. You can recognize male blooms because they have no tiny marrow behind them. Strip off the petals and twist the core of the male into the centre of a female flower. If the plants do not have sufficient water, not only may the marrows be on the woody side, but black fly is liable to infest the plants. Liquid manure feeds are also helpful. If you apply water and liquid feeds via clay pots sunk

eading Giant is an exceptionally ardy cauliflower for cutting in April

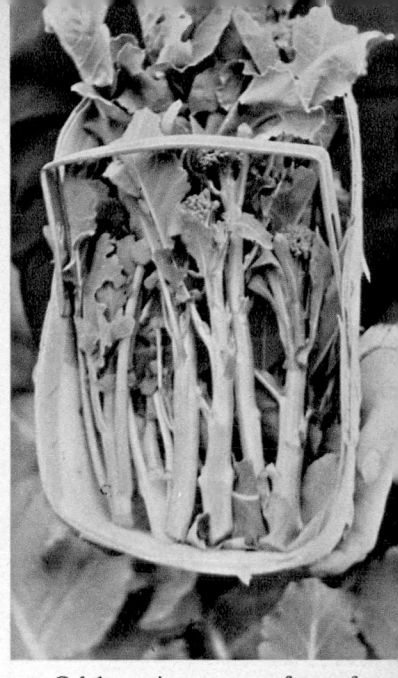

Calabrese is a summer form of sprouting broccoli

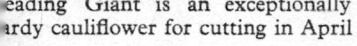

Cloches are a great help when it comes to ripening off the tomato crop

The wires on the trellis sag under the weight of the crop of
Outdoor Girl tomatoes

Golden Boy tomatoes have a fine flavour, and weigh up to 1 lb each

Sweet Peppers harvested from plants in the author's cold frame

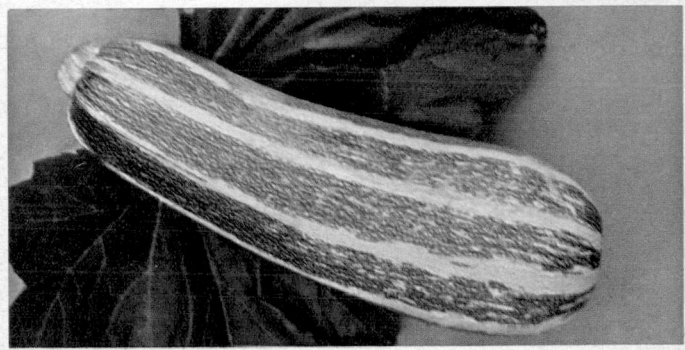

Sutton's Smallpak is a new bush type vegetable marrow

Save space by gardening vertically – you may need a stool
for harvesting vegetable marrows if you go too high!

FIG. 12(a) Strip the petals from a male flower and twist the core into the centre of the female, like this.

in the soil alongside the plants, you are sure that they reach the roots. Cut marrows when they are quite young. You should be able to pierce the skin with your thumb nail. Monster marrows may be gratifying to the gardener's pride, but are inferior in the pot. The more often you cut, the more marrows you will harvest. The plants come into bearing in late July and continue cropping until late September.

The vegetable marrow is very prone to an attack of Cucumber Mosaic Virus. Aphids are believed to be the distributors of

FIG. 12(b) Water and liquid feeds may be applied via clay pots
sunk alongside the plants

the virus. The first signs of this trouble are yellow streaks on
the leaves. These increase until the complete plant is yellowish,
stunted and unable to crop. Pull up and burn any plant which
shows the first signs of the virus.

Pumpkins. These are raised and treated exactly as if they
are trailing vegetable marrows. Bear in mind that pumpkin
shoots may reach a length of 10 ft and the leaves are very large.
I mention these points because it is no use going in for pumpkin growing unless you have ample room. Each plant sets one or
two fruits. You can hand pollinate if you wish. Feed with
liquid manure when the first pumpkins start to swell. Harvest
on a dry, sunny day in late September. Pumpkins keep well in
store, provided the storage place is cool and dry.

Varieties. Vegetable Marrow:

Bush	Trailing
Sutton's Smallpak	Sutton's Table Dainty
Zucchini F.1 Hybrid	Long Green Trailing

Pumpkin: Dobie's Mammoth.

For courgettes – see Chapter XIV.

CHAPTER XIV

THE EPICURE'S CHOICE

To my way of thinking, vegetable gardening is a dull job if you simply continue to grow the more usual vegetables without bothering to branch out a bit. In Part 1 no more than two of the vegetables covered in this chapter are included in the sample seed order and I repeat what I said earlier on: 'grow no more than one or two of them each season'. Some of them you may already know. By growing one or two each season, you will discover which of them you and the family like. The favourites will then be grown each year as a matter of course. Just because these vegetables are not seen in the neighbours' gardens, do not think that any special knowledge is needed to grow them. Provided you can grow the usual vegetables well, there is no difficulty at all with less usual kinds. They certainly help to vary the family's diet without resorting to the tin opener!

Globe Artichoke

This is the plant whose fat segments you may have nibbled in restaurants. The part that is eaten is the unopened flower and the plant is a handsome one in its own right, so that it is a fit subject for the herbaceous border.

Globe artichokes can quite easily be raised from seed, but I do not advise this because the plants are liable to be different from the original parents – however good they may have been. You need plants which produce large, fat, tight buds and it is better to buy growing plants from a good nursery. Gros Camus de Bretagne does this, but nobody in Britain appears to offer plants. My own plants are Gros Vert de Laon, which most people seem to think is the best.

Set the plants 3 ft apart in April and choose a sunny position. They need a reasonably fertile soil and one which is quite free of perennial weeds. Mulch with rotted manure or garden compost after planting. Repeat this mulch in May in future years. The plants may not crop in the first summer. They will in the second and third, after which it is advisable to start again with fresh plants. Keep the plants well watered if the summer is dry and feed with liquid manure. Cut off the dead foliage and spread a little bracken or straw over the crowns.

The buds are cut for use in July or August when they are fleshy and just before they start to break open.

New stock for a fresh start is easily obtained by detaching, with their roots, the young 'off-sets' at the base of the parent plants and replanting them immediately.

A few flower buds may, at your pleasure, be allowed to bloom. Flower arrangers are very keen on the mauve, thistle-like flowers, which sell at 2/6d each.

Beans for the Connoisseur

For those readers who are keen on trying less usual beans the general instructions on the growing of dwarf and runner beans (Chapter VI) cover seed sowing and cultivation. Compared with Continental suppliers, British seedsmen offer seed of *very* few varieties.

Grow as dwarf French beans: Royalty, Cherokee, Mont D'or, Speckled Cranberry, Deuil fin précoce, Fin de Bagnols.

Grow as dwarf French beans but allow the pods to ripen on the plants before shelling as dry haricots: Comtesse de Chambord, Brown Dutch, Mexican Black.

Grow as runner beans: Blue Coco, Blue Lake, Kentucky Wonder.

Grow as runner beans and harvest the seeds in the pods as fresh or dry haricots: Pea Bean Bicolor du Pape.

Grow as runner beans but allow the pods to ripen on the plants before shelling as dry 'Butter Beans': The Czar, White Wonder.

Capsicums

There are two kinds of Sweet Peppers or Capsicums. The first needs glass protection and produces a fine crop of large green peppers for stuffing or frying. The other is hardy enough for outdoor growing in the south.

For either type, sow seeds in pots in the cold frame or under a cloche in mid-April. In the north, I feel that it may be necessary to raise the plants in a slightly heated greenhouse. Thin the seedlings to leave one in each pot and plant out in early June.

The less hardy kinds grow to a height of almost 2 ft, so you need a tall frame or rather high cloches. Each plant needs 2 ft of space in the row. The hardier, dwarf plants need no more than a square foot of ground.

Except for weeding and watering little in the way of cultivation is necessary. Plants under glass benefit from being sprayed with clean water in warm weather and the glass should be flecked with whitewash in hot, sunny weather to prevent scorch.

Pick the peppers regularly as soon as they are full sized and keep on picking until late September.

Celeriac

Celeriac is a close relative of celery and the turnip-shaped roots, when grated, may be used as celery in soups and salads. The plants need a long growing season and seeds should be sown in a heated greenhouse in mid-March.

Sow in peat pots and sink them in a shallow trench in the greenhouse border. Thin the seedlings to leave one in each pot and harden off in the cold frame in early May. Plant out in mid-May at 1 ft apart. The soil should be really fertile but not recently manured. Do not plant deeply and remember that just as celery likes plenty of water, so does celeriac. Remove any sideshoots and suckers.

In the south, the roots may be dug when required for use; in colder parts, lift all of the crop in late October and store in sand or dry soil in the garden shed.

Chicory

There are different kinds of chicory so make sure that you start off with the right one. This is Witloof (Flemish for 'White Leaf'). Although considered as somewhat of a luxury, chicory is so easy to grow that I recommend it as a winter luxury to be eaten as a salad or braised to accompany meat or poultry.

Wait until mid-June in the south, early June in the north, before sowing the seeds rather thinly in inch deep seed drills, a foot apart. If the soil is dry, fill the drills with water before you sow. Hoe to keep down annual weeds and thin the plants to 9 in apart when they are about 2 in tall. No further cultivation is necessary. Even weeding is not necessary if you mulch the plants with sedge peat in late July.

In November, dig up all of the parsnip-like roots. Discard any which are thin or fanged and stand the rest in a trench. Pack earth around the roots and cover the trench with some straw. They can then be lifted a few at a time to be started into fresh growth and blanched.

Pull out a few roots, cut back any foliage that is left to an inch above the crown and reduce the length of the roots by an inch or two. Use the cabbage dibber to make holes very close together in the greenhouse border. Fill the holes with water and, when the water has drained away, plant a chicory root in each hole. Cover the crowns with an inch layer of dry straw and weigh this down by shovelling *dry* soil on top.

In a warm greenhouse, chicons will form within a month; in an unheated house, longer. Inspect the bed occasionally to check if any chicons are ready. When they are, remove the soil and straw and cut the chicons with a sharp knife. Compare their flavour with that of imported chicory.

If you have no greenhouse, blanch in a similar manner in the cold frame.

Chinese Cabbage and Chinese Mustard

I find both of these difficult. If you are successful, you may feel rather proud of yourself.

From my own results, I consider the new F.1 Hybrid Wonder Cross (seeds offered by George Roberts of Faversham) the best among the cabbage varieties. The plants make a loose head. Some people like to chop up the leaves in salads. I prefer to boil it as cabbage. Pac-Choy mustard resembles spinach after boiling.

Neither the cabbage nor the mustard is frost-hardy and, if sown before late June, the plants are liable to bolt. Make the seed drills 1 in deep and a foot apart and flood with water if the soil is dry. Sow thinly and firm gently with your boots afterwards. Thin the seedlings of the cabbage to 15 in and the mustard to 12 in. Should the roots find themselves short of water, the plants will bolt at once. From a late June or early July sowing, the crops will be ready for use in September.

Courgettes

It is not until you have enjoyed courgettes fried with bacon that you understand why the British public is rapidly becoming courgette-conscious. The courgette is simply an immature vegetable marrow and seeds are sown and plants grown in exactly the same way as those of bush-type vegetable marrows (see previous chapter). Seeds of a variety called Courgette are on sale. Zucchini F.1 Hybrid is just as suitable. Cut the courgettes two or three days after pollination of the female flowers. It is very important to pick regularly so that the plants keep on producing throughout the summer. For a good supply, grow two plants.

When going on holiday, arrange with a neighbour to harvest

and enjoy your courgettes; otherwise you will return home to find large vegetable marrows – and no more courgettes.

Endive

When properly blanched, endive replaces lettuce in autumn and winter salads. Sow in June. Sowing and cultivation is as for chicory.

The first batch of plants may be blanched as soon as the plants reach their full size. I have tried several blanching methods. The only satisfactory method is by digging up the plants and replanting under large clay pots. One plant under each pot. The plants must be perfectly dry at the time. Cover the drainage holes of the pots with slate or bricks. Unless blanched in absolute darkness, endive tends to remain bitter. The process takes from four to six weeks. Once blanched, endive must be used at once before it starts to rot.

Moss Curled chicory has finely cut and curly foliage while Batavian is broad-leaved and hardier.

Garlic

All kinds of claims for the health-giving qualities of garlic have been made over the past 2,000 years and some of the claims are recognized as valid today. You cannot fail to succeed with this crop. Simply bury the scales split off a garlic bulb, 2 in deep, 6 in apart with a foot between the rows. Hoe to prevent annual weeds and dig the crop in August when the foliage yellows. Dry off in the sun and store in trays in a frostproof shed or garage.

Kohlrabi

This odd-looking vegetable is, like the turnip, a cabbage with a round, swollen stem, but the swelling is wholly above ground. It has a mild turnip flavour.

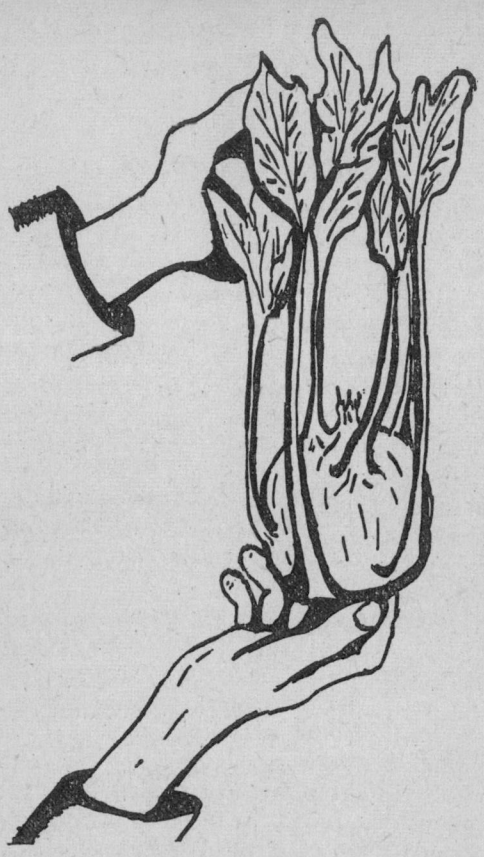

FIG. 13 Kohlrabi

Sow the seeds at any time between late March and July in inch deep drills spaced a foot or so apart. Thin the seedlings to 6 in apart as soon as you can. This is very important. If not thinned early, the plants bolt. They will also bolt if you keep them short of moisture, so water well and often in dry seasons

Harvest them when they are of cricket ball size. Green kohlrabi is tastier than the purple. If you keep rabbits, kohlrabi is worth growing because the rabbits will eat all of it – roots and foliage.

Cantaloupe Melons

The cantaloupe melon is a popular frame and cloche crop among south of England epicures. The plants are raised from seeds sown in pots in slight heat in early April or in the cold frame later that month. Transplant the seedlings into frames or under cloches in early June. Under barn cloches, allow 2 ft of row space per plant; in the cold frame 2 sq ft each.

Melons thrive in good garden soil and, providing the pruning of the plants is understood, this is not a difficult crop at all. Precautions must be taken to prevent stem rot which is caused by water lodging around the crown of the plants. To prevent the trouble set the plants on a slight ridge or hump, and leave a half-inch of the soil ball protruding above the ground. For watering and feeding purposes, sink a small clay pot on either side of each plant.

After planting, allow the plants to settle down for a week before you pinch out the growing point. Within a fortnight, the sideshoots which result from this action will have made several leaves. Only two shoots are required and these are pinched back to four leaves. Pinch off any other unwanted growth. Leave the plants to make a jungle-like growth of weak shoots in July.

To allow bees and other insects to pollinate the female flowers, remove a cloche or prop up the frame light on warm, sunny days. As soon as you see two or three melons about the size of small chicken eggs, it is time to prune once again. Retain no more than two, three or possibly four fruits on each plant. How many you leave depends on the final size of the melons. Two is enough on plants of large-fruiting kinds; three or four on small-fruiters.

Handle the immature melons very gently. Raise them on to

pieces of wood, tile or slate to keep them away from slugs. Then cut back the shoots to the *second leaf beyond each fruit.* Prune back all other growth to the second leaf beyond the original two main laterals.

In bright, hot weather shade the plants by flecking white-wash on the glass to give temporary shade with a piece of old lack or nylon curtain. During the few weeks when the fruits are swelling, water often and feed with liquid manure. As soon as a melon on a plant stops swelling, stop watering that plant. To discover when the first melon is ripe and ready for use, be guided by your nose. The sweet smell of a ripe melon fills the frame or the cloche row.

Varieties. Large fruits: Dutch Net, Tiger.
Medium: No Name.
Small: Sweetheart, Milky.

Peas for the Connoisseur

Asparagus Pea. This is not a member of the pea family but it does bear good crops of rather oddly-shaped, light green pods which are delicious if harvested when no longer than 1 in. If left on the plants, the pods become dreadfully stringy. Sow in early May in the manner of dwarf beans. Cloche protection is necessary in most parts of the country. If the plants appear too crowded, thin them out a little. A few twigs poked into the soil around the plants will prevent their toppling on to the soil.

Petits Pois. The variety Gullivert is on offer here. Grow as ordinary garden peas, pick on the young side and cook them on the same day.

Sugar Pea or Mangetout. Sow in May and treat as ordinary garden peas but expect the plants to reach a height of from 4 ft to 6 ft. Pick the pods *before* the seeds begin to swell inside them. The pods are cooked whole.

Salsify, Scorzonera, Hamburgh Parsley

The cultivation of these three root crops and the method of cooking them is so similar that I have decided to put them together here. They are reputed to have delicate flavours and, although I may be accused of iconoclasm, I think it fair to say that I prefer the parsnip. Grow them yourself and see what you think of them.

Salsify is rather like a short, rather narrow parsnip. Scorzonera roots are very thin, straight and almost black. Hamburgh Parsley roots could be mistaken for parsnips with a parsley foliage which may be used for garnishing.

Sow the seed in April. Sowing and cultivation are as for parsnips (see Chapter IX). Hamburgh Parsley needs as much water as celeriac. Start lifting the roots for use in October or November.

Seakale

This agreeable vegetable, of which one cooks the young, blanched shoots, can be raised from seed, but it is easier and quicker to buy a few thongs – which are root cuttings. If you have any difficulty in buying them, contact Suttons of Reading.

Plant in a sunny position on rich soil in March. If you can manure the bed with seaweed, so much the better. Make dibber holes at a foot apart, 18 in between rows, and plant so that the top of the cut root is $\frac{1}{2}$ in below the surface, making sure that the end of the thong with slanting end is lowermost. Mulch with well-rotted, strawy manure or garden compost in May. Keep the plants moist in dry spells and feed with liquid manure.

Allow the foliage to die off naturally and in November start blanching. The easiest way of doing this is to surround a part of the bed with planks or boxes and to cover the ground where the plants are with autumn leaves to a depth of a foot. Blanch another batch in November, December or January.

Squashes

There are two kinds of squash – summer and winter. Our English vegetable marrow is a summer squash. Raise seeds and cultivate as for vegetable marrow. There are bush and vining varieties. Here are a few you may like to try:

Custard Marrow (bush), Argentine Marrow (bush), South African Marrow (trailing), Summer Crookneck (bush), Giant Straightneck (bush).

Cook them just like vegetable marrow.

Most winter squashes are trailers. Raise seeds and cultivate as for pumpkins, although the plants do not need so much room. Harvest the attractive fruits in the late autumn and store for winter use in a cool, airy, frost-free, dry room. To enjoy cooked winter squash you need an American or Canadian wife who knows how to cook it!

Here are a few of the many varieties: Butternut, Golden Delicious, True Hubbard, Sweet Nut.

Sweet Corn and Popcorn

Sweet Corn is a form of maize and although a cereal is considered as a vegetable by the gardener. At one time it was considered a chancy crop. This is not so now that new, early maturing varieties have been developed and I particularly recommend the British F.1 hybrid, Kelvedon Glory. Given cloche protection throughout June, the plants should do well even in colder areas. Near the coast it may be necessary to erect a windbreak to protect the top-heavy, tall plants of Sweet Corn from wind damage.

Sow two or three seeds in peat pots during April (early April in Cornwall, mid-April in other parts of the south, later in April as you go north) and remove the weaker seedlings to leave one to grow on. Take off the cloches (or leave the frame light open) to harden off the plants before setting them out in early June, but hardening-off is not necessary if the plants are to receive continued cloche protection.

The plants are not grown in straight lines but in block formation because this encourages a good set of grains on the cob, the pollen being air-borne to the female. The actual spacing between the plants in the block should be about 18 in – no more. Four or five short rows make a good block. The soil must contain plenty of organic matter – rotted animal manure, garden compost, spent hops and the like. The plants need quite a lot of water, too, so that they make rapid growth during July and plump kernels in August. Any weeds should be pulled out by hand. A straw mulch laid down in July saves weeding and watering.

The cobs, which are covered in a leafy sheath, are ready for harvesting between early August and early September, depending on the weather. Do not twist off a cob until the 'silks', which droop from the cob, are shrivelled, dry and black or dark brown. The test for maturity is to strip off a part of the sheath and to press a grain with the thumbnail or a penknife. If the juice exuded is water, it is too early; if milky-cream, it is just right; if hard, it is fit only for chickens.

In the south it is possible to have a later supply of cobs by sowing in the open in mid-May, but if August is a cold month, results may be poor.

Popcorn. Sow, plant and cultivate just as if the plants were those of Sweet Corn. The difference in treatment occurs at harvesting. Whereas with corn-on-the-cob we seek freshness and succulence, with Popcorn we want hard, dry grains. The plants will die in September. Wait until the end of that month before harvesting on a dry, sunny day. If the weather remains dry, continue the drying process by hanging the cobs in the open. In wet weather, dry under cover. When the grains are very dry indeed, rub them from the cobs into a tray. Store the tray in a warm room for a few weeks before you start to pop the corn. This is something the children really enjoy.

CHAPTER XV

HERBS

THE vegetables we grow and the weeds which grow without our help are all herbs. There are, however, plants known as medicinal and pot herbs. We are not really a herb-conscious nation so this chapter will be confined to the few herbs I grow plus a few with which I am familiar.

Chives. This member of the onion family is grown for its tender leaves in spring. They may be used (chopped into small pieces) to flavour salads, sandwiches, stews, soups and omelettes. Plant small portions split from a large clump. Set them 9 in apart in March. They make an attractive edging plant. Weed and hoe occasionally. Cut the leaves with scissors when required for use. When the clumps get rather large, lift them in March, split them into smaller portions and replant.

Horse Radish. The plants need a well dug, well manured soil. Plant the roots a foot apart, using the spade or a dibber, so that the top of the root is just below soil level. In November, dig up *all* of the roots and store in a box of sand or ashes in the garden shed. Select a few straight roots for planting in the following March. Horse radish growing on waste land may also be dug and eaten.

Mint. Spearmint (*Mentha longifolia*) is generally grown. Many epicures prefer Apple Mint (*M. rotundifolia*) and so do some gardeners because the plants are not liable to suffer from an attack of a disease called Rust.

For reasons best known to the plants, mint flourishes like a weed in some places and refuses to grow in others. Your soil may be ideal, so, to prevent the mint from invading the garden, construct a special bed. Make a foot-deep trench around the site, line the sides of the trench with black polythene sheeting and replace the soil. Plant the roots in autumn or spring. Untangle them and lay them in inch deep drills. Mint may also be propagated from cuttings. Do not harvest any foliage in the first summer after planting.

Replant on a new bed when plants in the old bed become too crowded.

Parsley. Treat parsley as an annual. Sow in April and again in August in drills which are no more than $\frac{1}{2}$ in deep. The seeds take quite a time to germinate. Thin the seedlings to 6 in apart. Transfer some of the thinnings from the August sowing to the cold frame and set the light in position in October. Protect the other plants with cloches or keep your fingers crossed that they will not be severely damaged during the winter. Hoe and weed when necessary. Moss Curled is generally preferred. Here again, the plants make an attractive edging plant alongside the path.

Sage. The bushy shrubs prefer a light, well-drained soil. The dwarf, broad-leaved, non-flowering kind is the best. Set the plants 1 ft apart in April. When established, you may pick leaves or young shoots from June on.

Sage for drying should be picked in late June, using an airy place to prevent mildew. The bushes are considered worn out after 3 or 4 years. Replace them with younger bushes raised from cuttings taken in May or September. The cuttings may be as short as 2 in and, at the base, should have a small part of the main stem from which they are cut or plucked. When the cuttings are 5 in tall, nip out the growing point to induce branching.

Thyme. Common or Black thyme and Lemon thyme make

foot-high bushes. Plant and cultivate as for Sage. The soil may need a dressing of lime.

Laxton & Bunyard Nurseries, Brampton, Huntingdon, offer seeds and plants of many useful and interesting herbs. If you are interested, I suggest you write for a price list.

PART THREE

This section is a continuation of Chapter V in Part 1. Two of the chapters are aimed at helping readers to make use of an *existing* greenhouse for food crops or to grow something to eat where the garden is of pocket-handkerchief size.

Pests and Diseases have been pushed to the back of the book purposely. It would be a catastrophe to place the chapter elsewhere. Although the good gardener should be prepared to meet and recognize signs of trouble on his plants, he should not expect them as a matter of course. In the well cultivated kitchen garden, onslaughts by pests and diseases are rare. The gardener may not be an entomologist but he must be able to recognize the good and the few rather naughty insects in the garden.

CHAPTER XVI

FOOD CROPS IN THE SMALL GREENHOUSE

TOMATOES – TROUBLES – CUCUMBERS – MELONS AUBERGINES – FORCING RHUBARB

SMALL greenhouses are springing up like mushrooms in suburban gardens and I hope their owners get as much profit and pleasure from their purchases as I do from my own 8 ft × 6 ft cold house. Although most small greenhouses seem to be used mainly for ornamental plants, there is no reason at all why space should not be found at some time during the year for food crops. The general management of heated and unheated greenhouses and the cultivation of out-of-season vegetables is covered by Mr. H. Witham Fogg in his *The Small Greenhouse* – another Pan Piper book. In this chapter it is presumed that the gardener is using no form of artificial heat at all except, perhaps, for a small paraffin heater during April and May. No form of artificial heat is used in my greenhouse but, in the north, a paraffin stove prevents any risk of frost damage at night in the early part of the season.

It would not be wise to invest in a greenhouse without having first had a few years' practice in the craft of gardening. At any rate – that is my opinion. One starts with the growing of plants in the open and one advances to cloche cultivation and from cloches to the cold frame. From experience gained in dealing with plants under cloche and frame conditions, one knows quite a bit about ventilation and watering. These arc so vitally important – as one finds out when one embarks on greenhouse cultivation.

It is a great disappointment to me as a gardener when I see a fine, small greenhouse used to house an assortment of pot plants throughout the year. During the summer, many of them would be happier in the cold frame or sunk in the soil outdoors. It is obvious that the greenhouse owner either knows very little about greenhouse management or he simply hasn't the time to spare, so that his investment is not put to best use. It must be clearly understood that although all gardening is unnatural, greenhouse conditions are even more unnatural – as far as plant life is concerned. Before embarking on using the greenhouse for food plants, decide whether you will be able to give the growing plants that daily attention they require during the summer. During your summer holiday at the sea, make arrangements with a neighbour (preferably one who knows something about gardening) to carry out any routine jobs – particularly watering and ventilating.

The greenhouse border. If plants are grown in the greenhouse border they need less attention than if in pots. It is very important, however, that the soil in the border should be of good quality and, if your own is not up to standard, a good loamy topsoil should be ordered from a reliable source. Really first-class drainage is also essential and if, when removing the first spit, stiff clay is encountered, go down a foot deeper and mix gritty sand, reasonably small brick rubble or even stones into the clay. Although greenhouse-grown plants may need a lot of water, they do not care to find themselves standing in it. A little lime in the form of ground chalk may be sprinkled over the surface of the bed during the autumn. The border should then be flooded with water. Leave the door and the light wide open for a few days afterwards.

Tomatoes

My greenhouse is in use for food crops on and off from January until December, but the season starts in April when tomato seeds are sown. To prevent root disturbance, the plants are raised in peat pots. The pots are filled with sifted garden

FIG. 14
The small peat pots are filled with a suitable compost.
The plants are set in larger pots in May

compost (John Innes Seed Compost is also suitable), which is
firmed and watered. The smallest type of peat pot is used and
they are stood in seed trays. Two or three seeds are sown in
each pot and the tray is stood on the staging.

A temperature of 70°F is needed for good germination so,
in colder areas, some artificial heat may be of help. After
germination, the seedlings are satisfied with day temperatures

of between 60-65°F. Providing the greenhouse is frost-proof the young plants are not affected by low night temperatures.

Reduce the seedlings to one in each pot and when the size of the plants indicates that more space for root growth is required, set each small pot into a larger peat pot. Sink the pots fairly closely together in the border.

It may be thought that the warmer and wetter the conditions, the happier the small tomato plants will be. This is not the case. Ventilation must be adequate and it is only with experience and by using common sense that one gets to know when to ventilate and when to water.

Instead of raising your own tomato plants from seeds, you may prefer to buy a few plants from a nurseryman or shop during the last two weeks of May. This certainly saves work, but it may mean that you will have no choice at all as regards the variety.

Whether the young plants are the nurseryman's or your own, plant them out in the greenhouse border at the end of May, 18 in apart, and provide them with stakes.

Tomatoes need plenty of food, so the border should have been manured or composted earlier in the spring. Cultivation hereafter is as for tomatoes in the open (see Chapter XII) except that the plants may be allowed to produce up to six trusses instead of three or four, when the growing point is pinched out. If a proprietary liquid fertilizer is used, follow the manufacturer's instructions carefully, so that the plants are not over-fed.

Ring culture. More was heard about this new idea in tomato growing a few years ago than recently. It is certainly ideal where the soil in the greenhouse is diseased or pest-ridden. The soil itself is replaced by what is termed an 'aggregate' which may be vermiculite, breeze-clinker or coarse ashes. The plants are grown in bottomless whalehide pots filled with John Innes No. 3 compost. After planting, normal watering is carried out in the bottomless pots or 'rings' until the roots enter the aggregate. From then on the aggregate is watered daily but *not* the compost in the rings, but regular liquid feeds of a proprietary tomato fertilizer are applied *to the rings*. I have not grown tomatoes by this method, but from reports I have received it is apparent that the aggregate is liable to become sour after a few years and must be changed or washed well.

Troubles

Tomato Leaf Mould is a common trouble on greenhouse-grown plants. The older leaves are the first to be affected. Pale spots appear on them, and on the undersides of the spots, the mould develops. The spores quickly spread to other plants. A warm, stuffy atmosphere suits the fungus, so make sure that the house is well ventilated. Pick off and burn all affected leaves as soon as you see signs of Leaf Mould. From May on, give the plants some shade in bright, sunny weather. Green Polyglaze is useful because you may pin it in position or take it down so easily.

Varieties. Those who raise their own plants from seed should choose a variety for its flavour, such as Ailsa Craig (red) or Golden Boy (yellow-gold), instead of the overdone Money-maker.

Cucumbers

Wait until mid- or late April before sowing cucumber seeds. Improved Telegraph or Conqueror are varieties I can recommend. Sow two or three seeds in each $3\frac{1}{2}$ in peat pot filled with a suitable compost such as suggested for tomatoes. There is room for no more than three or four plants in the small greenhouse and, because of the humid atmosphere the plants need, do not try growing cucumbers and other food crops in the greenhouse at the same time. Sink the pots in the border and thin out the seedlings to leave one per pot.

Instead of raising from seed, one may buy seedlings for planting in the greenhouse in late May or early June. Do make sure, however, that you are sold plants of the right kind. Some shop assistants do not know much about what they are selling and the gardener finds he has been fobbed off with plants of the hardy, outdoor kinds. Set the plants 2 ft apart on the prepared bed.

In the old days, partially decayed stable manure was mixed with turfy loam and a special, rich, 18 in deep bed was made up on the greenhouse staging or in the border. If you have the manure and the loam, by all means follow this practice. If you haven't, I can assure you that by spreading a generous layer of ripe garden compost on top of the soil, you may expect an equally fine crop. When in bearing, the plants are watered or fed with liquid manure almost daily. This means that the drainage must be perfect.

A framework of wires or canes and wires is needed to which the plants may be tied. Stop the plants when they reach the top of the supports. Pinch out all sideshoots at the second leaf beyond the small cucumber on each of them. After being stopped in this way, the side shoots will produce lots of weaker shoots. Stop these in the same way. Remove all flowers on the main stem and pinch out as many male flowers as you can. You will recognize the males quite easily because they have no miniature cucumber behind them. It is an accepted belief that pollination of the female flowers results in seedy, misshapen and bitter cucumbers. That is why the males are removed.

Do not worry so much over ventilation as over watering, feeding and shading. The cucumber likes a Turkish bath atmosphere. In really warm weather, spray with tepid water each evening and damp the floor of the house. In July and again in August, top dress the bed with rotted manure or garden compost. This will encourage the production of new feeding roots on the main stem. Cut the cucumbers as soon as they are full-sized and cut often.

Prevention of Cucumber Foot Rot is an important aspect in

cucumber growing. The signs of this bacterial soft rot are brown markings at or above soil leading to the rotting of the main stem and the collapse of the plant. So set the plants on a slight mound to prevent water from lodging around the stem. Alternatively, leave 1 in of the soil ball protruding above the level of the bed at planting time and give all water and liquid feeds via a 5 in clay pot sunk in the soil alongside each plant.

Melons

Choose a hardy cantaloupe like Dutch Net or Tiger for cold greenhouse growing. Raise plants and set them out as for cucumbers. Stop all side shoots when a foot long and tie them to horizontal wires. Pinch out the growing point of the main stems when they reach the top of the supports.

The female flowers on the side shoots must be fertilized. Hand pollinate by transferring pollen from the males to the females, using a child's paint brush. The brush must be clean and dry. Do this on bright, sunny days at about noon. The female flowers carry an embryo melon at their rear.

When four fruits have set on each plant, cut off all surplus growth and start feeding with liquid manure. Water regularly, too, and pay as much attention to ventilation as with tomatoes. A top dressing of compost in July also helps. Take precautions at planting time against stem rot. If your melons grow as large as they should, they may tumble off the plants when almost ripe. Prevent this from happening by tying the melons in nets.

Aubergines (Egg Plants)

The Aubergine needs a long growing season and a really early start. This means the use of artificial heat when the seeds are sown in $3\frac{1}{2}$ in peat or clay pots in March. Transplant the seedlings at 18 in apart in the well manured or composted border during May. Pinch out the growing point of each plant to encourage branching. Prevent an infestation of red spider

FIG. 15 Pinch out the growing point of aubergine plants
to encourage branching

by spraying the plants of an evening with tepid water in July
and August. Cut the fruits when the 'eggs' are deep mauve and
somewhat soft. Long Purple is generally grown.

Forcing Rhubarb

To force rhubarb you need some plants and I do not suggest
that you dig up any of your own. I mention this because not all
gardeners know that, after forcing, the roots are quite worn out
and useless. A neighbour or a local grower may be replanting
and be able to supply you with what you need.

Plant the roots close together under the staging in January or
February. Water really well and drape a sheet of black polythene over the staging and down to the ground. This will
exclude most of the light. Water now and then. The tender

sticks will be ready for use several weeks before the main, outdoor crop. If your greenhouse has a heater in use at the time, the rhubarb will come along more rapidly.

FIG. 16 Black polythene helps with rhubarb forcing

CHAPTER XVII

POCKET HANDKERCHIEF GARDENS

SUITABLE VARIETIES – SPACE SAVING
WINDOW-BOX GARDENING

O NE of the sad things of present-day Britain is that gardens on many new housing estates are so small. These pocket-handkerchief sized gardens may suit the non-gardener, but one has but to take a walk through such an estate to see from the very many well-tended front gardens that the majority of the tenants are keen gardeners.

The keen gardener wishes to grow food crops, too. Both he and his wife wish their children to enjoy good food – and the best is produced in the garden. By the time a lawn is laid and the view from the living room and kitchenette windows cheered by a flower bed, there is precious little room for food crops. This chapter is aimed at helping the many keen gardeners who suffer from lack of garden space in the space age.

Decide first just how many square feet can be devoted to vegetables. The site should be unshaded and the small plot must receive intensive treatment. Intensive gardening calls for a very rich soil. First-class drainage is most important. This may mean the breaking up of some hard clay two spits down and the mixing into it of sharp sand and builder's rubble. Take care that the top soil does not get mixed into what lies below. After the digging, rake the bed level.

Nineteenth century intensive gardeners record the many tons of farmyard manure added as a surface mulch season after season until the whole bed resembled the rich black soil of the Ukraine – as it was, at any rate. For most of us there is little chance of loads of dung; however, some substitute must be found. Processed manure can be bought (at a price), turves can be stacked and rotted down for a year, roadside nettles can be gathered to be composted with other organic matter. If leaf mould is locally available it can be barrowed in or brought in by car in sacks. An annual mulch of soft leaves, especially oak or beech, is of great value.

Next, invest in a set of Barn cloches (either Low or Large Barns) and, if the space can be made for it, a cold frame. If you have any difficulty in getting these accessories, write to Expandite Limited, Downmill Road, Bracknell, Berkshire. Then consider what to grow.

Suitable Varieties

Where intensive methods are put into operation, rotation of crops is not practicable, although every effort must be made to avoid growing the same crop on the same spot within a year or two. Liming the soil may also be necessary regularly where the original soil below the compost is on the acid side.

The varieties of vegetables must be those that make little surplus leaf growth or that come into bearing without making tall plants which shade other plants near by. Sutton's Red Forcing radish makes short foliage and Tom Thumb lettuces need no more than 6 in of space. Early Nantes carrots are ready for use in June if sown with the lettuce and radish in late March or early April. Make this sowing under cloches and space the rows closely together.

Large, spreading cabbages are unsuitable. Sutton's April or Babyhead need little space. Spring onions for salads need little room and The Sutton broad bean is recommended for cloche growing or for small gardens. Dwarf French beans should not be forgotten and, if you wish to grow a runner, try Hammond's Dwarf Scarlet from Unwins.

For tomatoes that need no more than 12 or 18 in of space, I suggest the self-stopping bush varieties, Atom and Tiny Tim. There will be no room for potatoes, parsnips and winter cabbage, but space should be found for beetroot for summer salads and plants of Jade Cross brussels sprouts may be dotted between the lettuces or set alongside a row of first early dwarf peas like Forward or Histon Mini.

Bush type vegetable marrows are rather spreading, but Table Dainty, although a trailing variety, makes a short main shoot and the leaves are on the small side. I suggest that two plants of Table Dainty could be guided between rows of other plants without causing shade.

Space Saving

Gardening vertically, instead of horizontally, is another space-saving trick. Unattractive wire mesh fences may be made decorative and productive. If the fence is about 4 ft high, it pays to increase the height by 2 ft. This can be done effectively with some strong posts and wires, but Weldmesh is neater; the 2 in gauge is the best for vegetables. On such fences you may grow trailing vegetable marrows, hardy Japanese cucumbers and runner beans.

The same plants may also be grown on 'tripods' made from 8 ft bamboo canes fixed securely in the soil and tied together near the apex. Run some soft wire around them – from top to bottom – so that you have what looks rather like an openwork Indian wigwam. The bean plants will climb without your help but some tying-in will be necessary for marrows and cucumbers. Pinch out the growing points of the plants when they reach the top.

Intercropping, catch cropping and successional cropping (see Chapter IV) should be practised so that all of the small plot is used for several crops at the same time. Although your aim must be to grow the maximum number of plants, each of them must have sufficient room for development and all the light it requires. If space and light are denied, the plants will be weak and every pest in the neighbourhood will take up residence. From May until October, a supply of water must be at hand to ensure that there is no check to quick growth in dry spells. Mulching with straw, peat or black polythene will reduce the need for watering. The mulches will also prevent weeds from competing with the vegetable plants.

If you face this problem of shortage of space for food crops, a visit to the small Model Vegetable Garden in the grounds of the Royal Horticultural Society at Wisley, Surrey, is very much worth while.

Window-Box Gardening

I feel that the flat dweller needs a word of encouragement. Herbs are often recommended for growing in window boxes. I see no reason why small-scale vegetables growing should not be attempted in the same way. On a town flat balcony, large clay pots may also be of use for vegetables. I suggest Tom Thumb lettuce, Tiny Tim tomatoes and radishes in the window box. Standard type tomato plants, climbing cucumbers or even potatoes should do well in the pots.

For window boxes and pots you will need soil. Do not use any from a neighbour's garden; city soil is generally very acid. Either import some good top soil from a friend in the country or buy some John Innes Potting Compost at your local garden shop. You cannot build yourself a compost heap, so feed the growing plants with Liquinure or a similar fertilizer.

Mrs. Xenia Field deals with this subject more fully in *Window-Box Gardening* in this Pan Piper series.

CHAPTER XVIII

PESTS AND DISEASES

THE GARDENER'S FRIENDS – THE DARKER SIDE

ONE might well imagine the good gardener, armed with gas mask and spray gun, walking around the garden on the look-out for pests and diseases. That he doesn't is due to the fact that he does all possible to prevent pests and diseases. The soil is well fed and healthy, his rubbish is on the compost heap and not left around as a home for slugs and he practises rotation.

Song birds are welcomed throughout the year, but strawberries, other fruits and the vegetable seed beds are protected against bird damage. Weeds are suppressed because they harbour insects ready to damage growing crops. No large trees or tall fences cast shade which weakens the gardener's choice plants and sufficient water is given regularly when necessary.

If the garden is sited in an area where potato blight occurs frequently, the good gardener will spray *before* the plants show signs of the disease. The same watchful care prevents an infestation of black fly on bean plants and careful cultivation stops damage to carrots and onions by fly maggots.

The Gardener's Friends

Knowing the enemy is half the battle and the first lesson in control is to learn quite a lot about the many friendly insects, the birds and the occasional animal visitor we are likely to meet in the garden. Generally speaking, all quick-moving insects are on the good side of the fence. Even the ant, although he has a darker side, makes some excellent fine soil and very possibly takes part in pollinating melons, cucumbers and vegetable marrows.

Our best friend is the earthworm, which creates fertile soil, digs the garden, fertilizes it, drains it and aerates it. The earthworm is also able to mix top and subsoil together in a way we cannot hope to do. Earthworm farms in the United States breed worms for gardeners and farmers who need them in their soil. In Britain, the soil teems with earthworms which will stay with you and increase in numbers providing you feed them. Rotted manure and home-made garden compost suit them and keep them busy. Factory-made chemicals may sour the soil and cause them to leave the garden.

The ladybird does her best to keep our gardens free of aphids – black fly and green fly. American gardeners buy ladybirds by the gallon to clear up aphids in their gardens and orchards. If we use chemical pesticides and fungicides we may unwittingly kill our own ladybird population. Larvae of the lacewing fly also eat aphids and rove beetles destroy grubs of the cabbage root fly. Wasps deal with small caterpillars, weevils, and flies as well as being a nuisance during the plum season.

There are more than 1,800 species of ichneumon flies in Britain. The female fly has the unpleasant habit (although useful to us) of laying her eggs on the top of or inside caterpillars. The eggs hatch and the grubs devour the caterpillars alive!

Readers interested in this subject cannot do better than buy a copy of *Beneficial Insects* published at 5/6d by the Ministry of Agriculture. Copies are sold by Her Majesty's Stationery Office.

Most birds should be welcomed. The seed-eating wood pigeon is an exception and sparrows can be a nuisance. The lizard, the grass snake, the toad and the hedgehog are of great value as controllers of soil pests.

Special mention must be made of the hive bee and of wild bees, which deserve our protection for their work as pollinators. Without them we would have little fruit and fewer vegetables.

The Darker Side

If you take over an old, weedy garden or if you have to make a start on waste or pasture land, expect to come across small, thin, yellow grubs. These are wireworms. In nature, they perform a useful job in eating weed and grass roots. Prevent them from eating the roots of your vegetables by killing any you find when digging.

The black or dark brown millipede which curls up like a watch spring when touched must not be confused with the quick-moving yellow or reddish-gold centipede. The centipedes eat other insects – the millipedes eat plants. Quite often the millipede gets the blame for damage he has not done. Bean seeds sown in cold soil will rot, and the rotting seeds make a fine breeding ground for baby millipedes. They did not cause the original trouble. You did that yourself by sowing too early!

Cutworms and surface caterpillars chew through the stems of plants. Pick out any found when digging. Hoeing also disturbs them. Slugs and snails can gobble up a row of seedlings in a night and be very dangerous to some full-grown vegetables also. They can be partially repulsed by one of the several slug killers on the market.

Aphids must be controlled. Not only do these black, mauve, grey and green flies weaken plants but they also transmit killing virus infections from plant to plant. Liquid pyrethrum is a good control.

Chemicals for the Garden published last year at only 1/3d by the Ministry of Agriculture, contains some helpful drawings to enable the gardener to recognize harmful insects. The booklet also urges gardeners to use the chemicals BHC and DDT with restraint. *Pest Control without Poisons* published at 3/-d by The Henry Doubleday Research Association, Bocking, Braintree, Essex, should be read by every gardener who wishes to make quite sure that he does not poison himself, his family, wild life and beneficial insects.

Pyrethrum and derris can be of great help in preventing and controlling pests, while sulphur and copper preparations will do the like for fungus diseases. Unfortunately, up to the time of writing, there appears to be no preparation which will deal with soil pests but will not harm other helpful and harmless creatures.

APPENDIX A

Month by Month

January. Continue digging of light soils in favourable weather. Never dig frozen or frosted soil. Place order for seeds and seed potatoes. Inspect plants over-wintering under glass. Water only if necessary and remove any dead or dying leaves.

February. Where necessary, dress dug soil with lime. Plant rhubarb. In the south, conditions may be suitable for sowing parsnips outdoors and for planting shallots. Set cloches over rows where seeds are to be sown in March.

March. Fork the soil lightly, break up clods and rake level. Sow lettuce, summer cabbage, radish, brussels sprouts, carrots, broad beans, peas, onions – under glass or outdoors if the weather is suitable.

April. Do all possible to control weeds by hand-pulling and hoeing. Sow seeds of hardy vegetables in the open and of less hardy vegetables under glass. Plant potatoes. Set out plants of cauliflower, cabbage and lettuce over-wintered under glass. Set out onion plants and plant onion sets. Pull rhubarb. Harvest sprouting and heading broccoli.

May. Take precautions against night frosts. Continue outdoor sowings. Thin seedlings where necessary. Hoe to control weeds. Set out plants of hardy vegetables raised under glass. Harden off plants of less hardy vegetables in frames or under cloches. Plant tomatoes in the cold greenhouse. Pull rhubarb, pick sprouting broccoli and cut spring cabbages.

June. Hoe and mulch to control weeds. Water where necessary. Set out plants of half hardy vegetables outdoors or under glass. Plant brassicas for late summer, autumn and winter supplies. Dust or spray broad beans with pyrethrum. Continue vegetable sowings. Thin seedlings. Earth-up potatoes. Continue collecting material for the compost heap. Dig first potatoes. Pick peas. Cut more spring cabbages. Pull rhubarb. Pull spring onions. Plant leeks.

July. Weed, mulch and water where necessary. Look out for pests and diseases. Continue vegetable sowings for succession. Make liquid manure. Feed vegetable marrow plants with liquid manure. In the north, sow spring cabbage. Earth up potatoes. Tie in tomato plants and remove side shoots. Dig potatoes. Pick peas, broad and dwarf beans. Pull young carrots and beet. Thin rows of vegetable plants where necessary. Harvest shallots. Shade plants under glass.

August. Weed and water where necessary. Continue digging potatoes as and when wanted. Feed melons, cucumbers and vegetable marrows. Harvest onions. Sow spring cabbage in the south. Sow lettuce and cauliflowers. Continue harvesting vegetables regularly. Pick tomatoes. Sow onions. Earth up celery.

September. Hoe where necessary. Set out spring cabbage plants. Cloche lettuce plants. Earth up celery. Cloche tomato plants. Harvest last tomatoes. Pick last runner beans. Cut autumn cabbages. Lift, dry and store onions and maincrop potatoes.

October. Harvest carrots and beetroot and store. Cut autumn cabbages. Clear up generally and add all vegetable debris to the compost heap.

November. Start digging or forking the soil. Add manure or garden compost. Plant rhubarb. Lift parsnips and swedes when required for use. Start blanching endive, chicory and seakale. Start forcing rhubarb crowns. Repair cloches, cold frame and greenhouse if necessary. Clean greenhouse, garden shed and tools. Inspect potatoes and roots in store. Remove any showing rot. Cut lettuces from under glass.

December. Finish all clearing up, digging and forking if weather permits. Spread straw over celery. Inspect potatoes and roots in store. Force rhubarb. Continue blanching. Write to seed firms for catalogues. Harvest cabbages and brussels sprouts. Dig up and harvest swedes. Dig parsnips when required for use. Enjoy Christmas!

APPENDIX B

Kitchen Garden Jargon

Acid Soil. Soil deficient in lime.

Alkaline Soil. Soil containing much lime.

Aphis, aphids. Plant lice: greenfly, blue fly, black fly.

Artificials. Chemical fertilizers.

Bacteria. One-celled forms of life.

Biennials. Plants which take about two years to complete their life cycle.

Blanching. Blanch. Blanched. To make white. Made white.

Bolt. Bolting. Bolted. Premature flowering, 'running to seed.'

Bordeaux Mixture. A fungicide containing copper and lime.

Border. A special bed for plants outdoors or in the greenhouse.

Brassicas. The cabbage plant family.

Burgundy Mixture. A fungicide containing copper and soda.

Calcium. A chemical element contained in chalk and limestone.

Catch Crop. A crop grown on a piece of land temporarily vacant.

Club Root. A fungoid disease of brassicas.

Compost. (a) A special potting mixture *or* (b) a manure made by fermenting waste materials.

Compost Heap. A pile of fermenting animal and vegetable wastes.

Crock. Drainage material used in clay pots and seed boxes.

Crown. The part of the plant which is at soil level or just above it. Generally a perennial.

Dibber. A pointed wooden tool for planting.

Double-dig. Digging to a depth of about 20 in without mixing the top with the subsoil.

Drill, seed drill. A shallow furrow made with the hoe.

Earth-up. Draw soil up and around plants.

Eye. Bud on a tuber, especially on potatoes.

Finger and Toe. See *Club Root.*

Forcing. Hastening plants to produce.

Fungicide. A powder or liquid to kill fungi.

Fungoid disease. Disease caused by the spores of fungi, as contrasted with attacks by insect pests.

Gall. A lump on a root or stem as made by Cabbage or Turnip Gall Weevil.

Haulm. Top growth of potatoes.

Head. Developed top growth of cabbage, cauliflower, celery, lettuce.

Heart; Heart-up. Centre of developed top growth of cabbage, cauliflower, lettuce. To develop a firm central part.

Heel-in. To plant temporarily in the ground. Not final planting.

Heavy Soil. One preponderating in clay.

Hop Manure. A manufactured product with hops as the base.

Humus. An organic constituent of the soil formed by the decay of organic matter; 'vegetable mould'.

*Hybrid – F.*1. A plant obtained by controlled fertilization of seed.

John Innes (J.I.) Composts. Seed and potting composts made according to formulae prescribed by the John Innes Horticultural Institute.

Legumes. Peas and beans.

Light. The top, removable part of a frame.

Light Soil. A soil containing much sand.

Lime. Chalk, limestone (calcium carbonate), quicklime (calcium oxide), slaked lime (calcium hydroxide).

Liquid Manure. Plant foods in water solution.

Loam. A good mixture of clay, sand and organic matter. Good
topsoil.

Mulch. A soil cover around plants.

Neutral Soil. Neither acid nor alkaline.

Organic. Matter originating from some order of creation having
the organs of life and growth.

Peat. Vegetable matter long decayed in waterlogged conditions.
Pinch-out. Stop growth of a shoot, using the fingers.
Plain Digging. Digging and turning the soil to the depth of the
spade – about 10 in.
Pot-on. Move a pot plant to a larger pot.
Potting. Setting a seedling or plant in a pot.
Prick-out. Set seedlings into other containers or into the open
ground at wider spacing than before.

Quick-Lime. Calcium oxide.

Ridging. Heaping the soil into ridges to expose it to wind and
frost action.
Rose. An attachment to a watering can for use when watering
seedlings; a 'fine' rose has very small holes.

Seed Drill. See *Drill.*
Seed Leaf. First leaf or first pair of leaves, usually different from
the 'true' leaf.
Set. Set-out. To plant.
Spit. Depth of a spade – 10 in.
Stop. Prevent further growth of stem or shoots by pinching out
growing point.
Subsoil. Soil below top soil.

Thin. Reduction of the number of plants in containers or in the soil.

Thinnings. Plants removed during the process of thinning.

Top-dress. To spread manure, compost, peat, leaves, etc., on the surface of the soil around growing plants.

Trace Elements. Chemicals vital to plant growth but needed in very small quantities.

True Leaf. Typical leaf of a plant; often different from seed leaves.

Tuber. A swollen underground stem as in the potato or Jerusalem artichoke.

Wilting. Flagging of leaves or of plant due to lack of water, to excessive heat or to disease.

APPENDIX C

Some Reliable Seedsmen

The following seedsmen have supported my vegetable trials here. Without their past and continued kind help this book could not have been written.

Alexander & Brown, Perth.

Carter's Tested Seeds Ltd., Raynes Park, London, S.W.20.

Samuel Dobie & Son Ltd., Grosvenor Street, Chester.

S. E. Marshall & Co. Ltd., Oldfield Lane, Wisbech, Cambs.

George B. Roberts, Faversham, Kent.

Ryders of St. Albans Ltd., Waltham Cross, Herts.

Sutton & Sons Ltd., Reading, Berks.

Thompson & Morgan (Ipswich) Ltd., London Road, Ipswich.

W. J. Unwin Ltd., Histon, Cambridge.

G. Winfield & Son Ltd., 26 Westgate Street, Gloucester GLNI 2NH.

INDEX